DRAWING
NEAR

A PERSONAL DEVOTIONAL
JOURNEY TO HIS HEART

Journal

— JOHN BEVERE —

D1621862

Drawing Near: A Personal Devotional Journey to His Heart
Copyright © 2004 by John Bevere

ISBN 0-9633176-9-5

Scripture passages taken from:

The Holy Bible: New King James Version (NKJV)
Copyright © 1982 by Thomas Nelson, Inc. Used by permission. All rights reserved.

The New King James Bible, New Testament
Copyright © 1979 by Thomas Nelson, Inc. Used by permission. All rights reserved.

The New King James Bible, New Testament and Psalms
Copyright © 1980 by Thomas Nelson, Inc. Used by permission. All rights reserved.

All rights reserved. No portion of this book may be reproduced, stored in a retrieval system, or transmitted in any form or by any means–electronic, mechanical, photocopy, recording, or any other–except for brief quotations in printed reviews, without the prior permission of the publisher.

Requests for information should be addressed to:
Messenger International
PO Box 888, Palmer Lake, CO 80133-0888
www.johnbevere.org

Project Management and Media Consultant: www.vaughnstreet.com

COVER & INTERIOR DESIGN:
Eastco Multi Media Solutions
3646 California Rd.
Orchard Park, NY 14127
www.eastcomultimedia.com

Compiler: Holt Vaughn
Editor: Debbie Moss
Design Manager: Jonathan La Porta
Designers: Jonathan La Porta, Aaron La Porta, Bryan Matthews

Printed in the United States of America

How to Use This Devotional Journal

Growing in your relationship with the Lord is about developing your passion, love, humility, and obedience. Using the book *Drawing Near* and your *Personal Devotional Journal* is very straightforward. **You simply read the book, watch the videos, and go through the devotional journal.**

Here are some detailed easy-to-use instructions:

• **There are twelve video sessions and twelve weeks of devotions and journaling.** Each week of the devotional journal is designed to take what you learn in the book and the videos and bring it to reality as you spend time with God Himself.

• **This is your personal journey, and it can be as flexible as you need it to be.** You may want to go through it as your daily time with God, but you don't have to. This is set up as a 12-week encounter (84 days of devotions, see pages 4&5 for Step by Step Instructions). You could start each morning or finish each evening with the devotional.

• **Or you can do it over a more extended period.** For instance, you could set aside a few days during the week, maybe a Tuesday evening and Saturday morning, and go through a few sessions each time. This journey can be done at any pace you desire.

• **The key is consistency.** Choose the schedule you'll follow, and then keep it faithfully. Life is full of changing circumstances, so if you miss some of your scheduled times, that's OK. No big deal. Just get back to it; pick up where you left off, and follow through to completion.

• **Set aside your quiet time**, preferably in a place where you and God can be together, uninterrupted.

Suggested Step by Step Instructions for a 12-week journey

Read the corresponding chapters in the hardback book, *Drawing Near*, watch the corresponding video session and then go through the seven days of that week in the devotional journal.

Week 1

- Read chapters 1 and 2 of *Drawing Near* hardback book
- Watch video *Session One*
- Go day-by-day through week 1 in your *Devotional Journal*

Week 2

- Read chapter 3 of *Drawing Near*
- Watch video *Session Two*
- Go day-by-day through week 2 in your *Devotional Journal*

Week 3

- Read chapters 4 and 5 of *Drawing Near*
- Watch video *Session Three*
- Go day-by-day through week 3 in your *Devotional Journal*

Week 4

- Read chapter 6 of *Drawing Near*
- Watch video *Session Four*
- Go day-by-day through week 4 in your *Devotional Journal*

Week 5

- Read chapter 7 of Drawing Near
- Watch video *Session Five*
- Go day-by-day through week 5 in your *Devotional Journal*

Week 6

- Read chapter 8 of Drawing Near
- Watch video *Session Six*
- Go day-by-day through week 6 in your *Devotional Journal*

Suggested Step by Step Instructions for a 12-week journey

Week 7

- Read chapter 9 of *Drawing Near*
- Watch video *Session Seven*
- Go day-by-day through week 7 in your *Devotional Journal*

Week 8

- Read chapter 10 of *Drawing Near*
- Watch video *Session Eight*
- Go day-by-day through week 8 in your *Devotional Journal*

Week 9

- Read chapter 11 of *Drawing Near*
- Watch video *Session Nine*
- Go day-by-day through week 9 in your *Devotional Journal*

Week 10

- Read chapter 12 of *Drawing Near*
- Watch video *Session Ten*
- Go day-by-day through week 10 in your *Devotional Journal*

Week 11

- Read chapter 13 of Drawing Near
- Watch video *Session Eleven*
- Go day-by-day through week 11 in your *Devotional Journal*

Week 12

- Read chapter 14 of Drawing Near
- Watch video *Session Twelve*
- Go day-by-day through week 12 in your *Devotional Journal*

Welcome to Drawing Near,
A PERSONAL DEVOTIONAL JOURNEY TO HIS HEART

You are going to embark on a life-changing 12-week, 84-day encounter with God. The purpose of this devotional journal is to remove barriers that hinder you in your relationship with God and to take you deeper into intimacy with Him. You will be transformed as you read the book *Drawing Near*, go through the video sessions, and then use this devotional journal. This isn't just a 12-week experience; it is the launching pad to the exciting lifelong adventure that is available to everyone who makes the decision to live each day in intimacy with God!

You won't find a formula or step-by-step mechanical process here. Rather, you will find living, breathing interaction with God Himself!

As you take the initiative each day in these special one-on-one personal sessions, you can expect God to keep the promise in James 4:8: "Draw near to God and He will draw near to you."

You'll discover that God really does desire your company. You'll find treasure in the heart of God for your life and for the world around you as He speaks to you, leading and guiding you by His Word and precious Holy Spirit. Be prepared to be amazed at what you find in the next few weeks as you take this road of discovery to new realms of God's kingdom and your own heart.

One of the features of this devotional is that it includes "journaling." This may be new to you. Webster's dictionary defines journaling as "a record of experiences, ideas, or reflections kept regularly for private use." Consider this journaling as an important part of your daily time with God. In the Old Testament, God told His people to write things down, so they could be passed down from generation to generation. Of course, we have the New Testament for the simple reason that it was written down as a record of the words and works of Jesus and His disciples. We are to keep His words written upon our hearts, and journaling is an excellent way to accomplish this.

The following are not all hard and fast rules, but they are helpful suggestions for what to include in your journaling: *(see next page)*

- Always record the date and time.
- Write a brief review of the days events that are of importance/significance.
- Record feelings: good, bad, or indifferent.
- Make note of thoughts and images that the Holy Spirit brings before you (for example, working through a childhood experience or praying for someone at work).
- Write down Bible verses that come alive to you.
- Write down quotes from books you are reading that apply to your life today.
- Include things that come to mind that seem appropriate.
- Include pictures, newspaper articles, and other items of personal importance.
- Write what God tells and reveals to you each day, even if you do not fully understand it.

You'll quickly find that as you draw near to God, He will start speaking to you more than ever before! Therefore, you may want to start a journal of your own if you don't already have one to use in addition to the spaces provided in this devotional. You can use a simple spiral notebook, or you can find beautifully designed and bound journaling notebooks at many bookstores.

This spiritual journal will be an invaluable tool for years to come. Journaling will help you understand how God is working in your life as you see your progress and gain clarity in your walk with God. You will be able to look back and see the amazing works God has accomplished in your life as you've grown in intimacy with Him. It will be a great source of inspiration and faith. It will be a way to enable you to share with others the wonderful testimony of what God has done in your life.

Start today to experience a lifetime of intimacy with God!

Draw near to Him, and He will draw near to you!

Introduction & Welcome
The first time you watch the DVD, please choose the "Individual" path. You will be asked to enter the code below for a personal welcome from John

DVD Extra Feature Enter code: **564**, *to watch this bonus feature as you begin your journey.*

THE GREATEST INVITATION OF ALL TIME

"When I consider Your heavens, the work of Your fingers, the moon and the stars, which You have ordained, what is man that You are mindful of him?"
Psalms 8:3–4

"Draw near to God and He will draw near to you."
James 4:8

KEY STATEMENT: There is something I can do that will literally cause the One who put the stars in the universe to come near me.

This is it. You are here. You've purchased this devotional, and you're beginning. Right now, this very moment, it starts. But what does it mean? Is this just another fad or another attempt to be a "better Christian"? Will you actually finish it, or will it be left undone, incomplete? Pages never read, prayers, thoughts, feelings, victories, losses, pain, and joy never written, never recorded?

It doesn't have to be that way. This is not about becoming a "better Christian" or a better person. What starts right now is this: you are going to take the initiative, the first step down the road of this journey, directly to His heart—God the Father's heart, Jesus the Christ, the Holy Spirit Himself.

Take a cue from Psalms 8 above. Take a few moments and bend your heart toward God. Consider His heavens, the beauty of His creation, all the things that put you in awe of your Creator. Then worship Him for who He is. Don't worry about using fancy words; just be yourself. There is no need to edit your worship or your prayers.

Now look at James 4:8 above. This is the greatest invitation of all time. God has invited you to be with Him. And not just with Him, but near to Him. This same God promised that when you do this, He will place Himself near to you. It doesn't get any better than that. Lastly, simply tell Him how you really feel right now—the good, the bad, and the ugly.

Place a few thoughts about this first encounter in your journal, and don't forget to thank Him and tell Him you are looking forward to tomorrow.

_____

_____

_____

_____

Your Drawing Near journey begins with a saving relationship with Jesus. Turn to page 237 and read Appendix A ("Our Need for a Savior") in your Drawing Near book.

Enter code: **297**, to watch the bonus feature in the first session of your DVD.
(*Please note that this code is for the 2nd bonus icon in session 1, not the first icon.)

DVD Extra Feature

THE GREATEST INVITATION OF ALL TIME

"But God demonstrates His own love toward us, in that while we were still sinners, Christ died for us."
Romans 5:8

"For if when we were enemies we were reconciled to God through the death of His Son, much more, having been reconciled, we shall be saved by His life."
Romans 5:10

"Now that we have actually received this amazing friendship with God, we are no longer content to simply say it in plodding prose. We sing and shout our praises to God through Jesus, the Messiah!"
Romans 5:11, The Message

KEY STATEMENT: Can you imagine the Holy Spirit staying with us and not leaving us, even the way we behaved, and still drawing us to Jesus when we were still enemies?

Enemies of God. That's what we were before we became Christians. Whether we were raging, evil, and murderous or sweet, well-dressed, nice, and church-going, the bottom line is, when we were still sinners, it was in that condition that God saw us and loved us. At one point in His earthly ministry Jesus said that if we love those who love us we are no better than a sinner. It's when we love those who hate us that we please God. And that's what Jesus did for us. Regardless of how we looked on the outside, we were dead on the inside, and He brought us from death to life. And this life comes to us not because we deserve it. We've done nothing to merit it. It was He who came to rescue us even though we were His enemies.

Take a look at Romans 5:11 again. And like yesterday, take a cue from the Scriptures. Now that you've received this amazing friendship with God, don't be content with anything less than a lifetime of closeness with Him. Take a few moments or whatever time you need, meditate on these things, worship Him, and expect Him to draw near to you in the midst of your praises and prayers. If there is something between you and Him that is holding you back, now is the perfect time to deal with it—draw near to Him, and He will draw near to you.

Journal here anything that transpires between you and God at this time:

_____

_____

_____

_____

_____

_____

_____

THE GREATEST INVITATION OF ALL TIME

"For the Son of Man has come to seek and to save that which was lost."
Luke 19:10

"Here's a word you can take to heart and depend on: Jesus Christ came into the world to save sinners. I'm proof—Public Sinner Number One—of someone who could never have made it apart from sheer mercy. And now he shows me off—evidence of his endless patience—to those who are right on the edge of trusting him forever."
1 Timothy 1:15–16, The Message

(Written in a letter to a young preacher by a man whose name had been Saul and who was once a persecutor and murderer of followers of Jesus. Remarkably this same Saul had become forgiven and saved by Jesus. We know him today as the apostle Paul.)

KEY STATEMENT: Jesus came for you.

There is a story of the great Dr. Archibald Alexander, a professor of divinity at Princeton. After a distinguished career of sixty years of preaching, it is said that on his deathbed he made this statement to his friend: *"All my theology is reduced to this narrow compass; Jesus Christ came into the world to save sinners."*

This journey isn't necessarily about theological perfection or doctrinal debates. Even the most knowledgeable or distinguished among us becomes silent at the feet of this God who has given His very best that we might have life. In verse 10 of the tenth chapter of John's Gospel, Jesus Himself said that the very reason He came was to give us life. The words He used can be translated as abundant life or real and eternal life. One translation says, *"...more and better life than they ever dreamed of"* (The Message).

No matter who you are, no matter what you've done, this thing is personal. God gave His best so you could have eternal life. Tomorrow we'll go deeper into this subject. For now, thank God for how He has found you at this moment as you meditate on the wonder that He sent Jesus for you.

_____

_____

_____

_____

_____

_____

_____

THE GREATEST INVITATION OF ALL TIME

Week 1 Day 4

"...that the world may know that You have sent Me, and have loved them as You have loved Me."
John 17:23b

"I in them and you in me. Then they'll be mature in this oneness, and give the godless world evidence that you've sent me and loved them in the same way you've loved me."
John 17:23, The Message

KEY STATEMENT: Are we to understand that God loves us as much as God loves Jesus? YES!

It seems remarkable, doesn't it—maybe even too good to be true, like a fairytale or a movie, a Shakespearean play or a best-selling novel. But this epic adventure wasn't created from some man's or woman's imagination. The Creator Himself has revealed this eternal drama to us. You can find it in the Bible from Genesis to Revelation, but it doesn't stop there. It is revealed in the length and breadth of history and in the order of nature. You can see it in the lives of those who humbly but passionately call themselves disciples of Jesus. God really does love us with the same love He has for His Son!

Still struggling with this? Romans 10:17 gives us a remedy for our doubt. It says, *"Faith comes by hearing, and hearing by the word of God."*

- John 3:16: *"For God so loved the world that He gave His only begotten Son."*
- 1 Peter 2:24: *"Who Himself bore our sins in His own body on the tree...by [His] stripes you were healed."*
- 1 Corinthians 6:20 (NLT); Ephesians 1:7 (NLT): *"God bought you with a high price....He is so rich in kindness that he purchased our freedom through the blood of his Son."*
- Romans 5:8: *"But God demonstrates His own love toward us, in that while we were still sinners, Christ died for us."*
- Romans 5:10: *"For if when we were enemies we were reconciled to God through the death of His Son, much more, having been reconciled, we shall be saved by His life."*

For this devotional and journaling time, work out your feelings, letting God speak to you through the Scriptures and the Holy Spirit about the fact that God loves you in the very same way He loves His Son.

_____

_____

_____

_____

_____

_____

_____

_____

"We have been the recipients of the choicest bounties of Heaven. We have been preserved, these many years, in peace and prosperity. We have grown in numbers, wealth and power, as no other nation has ever grown. But we have forgotten God. We have forgotten the gracious hand which preserved us in peace, and multiplied and enriched and strengthened us; and we have vainly imagined, in the deceitfulness of our hearts, that all these blessings were produced by some superior wisdom and virtue of our own. Intoxicated with unbroken success, we have become too self-sufficient to feel the necessity of redeeming and preserving grace, too proud to pray to the God that made us!"

President Abraham Lincoln
-in a proclamation appointing a National Fast Day, March 30, 1863

KEY STATEMENT: People who emphasize the blessings of God to the neglect of a relationship with Him create disciples who come to God to get something, rather than those who respond to Him for who He is.

It was almost 150 years ago that Abraham Lincoln in all of his eloquence confronted an issue that remains a challenge to this day. Thousands of years ago it was a challenge too. History is replete with Romans, Greeks, and other civilizations that were choked by their own prosperity. When God delivered His people from generations of brutal, cruel slavery and brought them into the Promised Land that flowed with milk and honey, He repeatedly warned them never to forget Him no matter how much they flourished. They were to remember that it was He who freed them from bondage, and it was only because of Him that they had a new and abundant life. God was grieved when His people forgot Him for the "toys" He had blessed them with.

Here are some easy-to-remember phrases that will help us keep our priorities straight. Meditate on these, and write down a few of your own. Pray about and consider ways in which you may have fallen into this very trap.

We must seek:
- The Promiser, not the promise
- The Giver, not the gift
- The Creator, not His creation

_____

_____

_____

_____

_____

_____

THE GREATEST INVITATION OF ALL TIME

Week 1 Day 6

"But seek first the kingdom of God and His righteousness, and all these things shall be added to you."
Matthew 6:33

"What I'm trying to do here is to get you to relax, to not be so preoccupied with getting, so you can respond to God's giving. People who don't know God and the way he works fuss over these things, but you know both God and how he works. Steep your life in God-reality, God-initiative, God-provisions. Don't worry about missing out. You'll find all your everyday human concerns will be met."
Matthew 6:31–33, The Message, emphasis added

KEY STATEMENT: Relax; don't be so preoccupied with getting, so then you can respond to God's giving.

Western culture today almost rams it down your throat. Success is measured Hollywood style—beauty, fame, and cash flow. If you don't have an abundance of these, well, let's face it; you really don't have much worth at all. And so it creeps into the church, and before you know it, we have what we looked at in yesterday's devotions: a people who somehow lost their fascination and passion for their lover and instead became fascinated and passionate about their lover's gifts.

What a contrast this is to those who live in intimacy with the God who owns everything anyway. We learn to simply seek Him, and He cares for us, supplying not just our material needs but our deeper, eternal, spiritual, emotional and love-needs. First Peter 5:7 says, *"Casting all your care upon Him, for He cares for you."* Think of your life as God's garden, and He is the garden's caretaker. Having planted you in good soil, He provides the rain and sunlight. All you need is to grow and flourish and bear much fruit. Your job is simply to keep growing upward toward the sun.

Review yesterday's devotion, and remember we must seek the One who blesses, not just the blessings.

_____

_____

_____

_____

_____

_____

_____

_____

_____

_____

THE GREATEST INVITATION OF ALL TIME

*"Rejoice always, pray without ceasing, in everything give thanks;
for this is the will of God in Christ Jesus for you."*
I Thessalonians 5:16–18

"The most awful, living, reverend frame I ever felt or beheld, I must say, was his prayer. And truly it was a testimony. He knew and lived nearer to the Lord than other men, for they that know Him most will see most reason to approach Him with reverence and fear." [1]
So said William Penn of George Fox
(William Penn (1644-1718) was the famous English Quaker who founded Pennsylvania. George Fox (1624-1691), an English leader, founded the Quakers. Fox once told a British judge "to tremble at the word of the Lord.")

KEY STATEMENT: God isn't saying He wants to talk to you without ceasing, but rather He is willing to communicate without ceasing.

Prayer is not simply a monologue, but rather a dialogue. As a loving Father, God desires a continuing, two-way relationship of intimacy with His children.

A husband and a wife, mother and daughter, father and son—we've all seen it. People in these relationships can communicate whole paragraphs with a nod, a glance, a grunt, a touch, or a single gesture. We take it for granted, yet it's actually beautiful to behold—just ask someone who is alone and who has no one intimate with whom to share every nuance of life.

Thank God none of us are alone if we have Jesus. And that's what this journey to His heart is all about: a lifetime of intimate communication with God Himself. God wants to communicate with us just like the most intimate relationship we would have with a family member. Drawing near to God is not just about talking—saying many words. Remember, Jesus said in Matthew 6:7 that it is a mistake to think that we will be heard because of the multitude of our words.

Vain repetitions don't move God; relationship does. He has extended us an invitation to draw near, and now you are the one who determines your level of relationship with God, not God. *"For he is a God who is passionate about his relationship with you"* (Exod. 34:14, NLT).

If you have made it this far, you are serious about drawing near to God. You obviously know you have a part to play, and you are answering God's impassioned call to you. Take whatever time you need, and worship God and thank Him for all He has done this past week.

Jot down anything that has been important to you throughout this first week's journey. Let the Holy Spirit recap the events of the week and speak to you about the coming week. God wants to bless you in this relationship. Now give Him the opportunity to do it.

(Journaling space available on the next page.)

THE GREATEST INVITATION OF ALL TIME

Additional Notes

"My soul thirsts for God, for the living God. When shall I come and appear before God? My tears have been my food day and night, while they continually say to me, 'Where is your God?' When I remember these things, I pour out my soul within me."

Psalms 42:2–4

KEY STATEMENT: We will hunger for what we feed on.

FEET TO OUR FAITH: SCRIPTURE MEMORIZATION *"This Book of the Law shall not depart from your mouth, but you shall mediate in it day and night, that you may observe to do according to all that is written in it. For then you will make your way prosperous, and then you will have good success" (Joshua 1:8).*

"WORK!? You mean I'm going to have to do some work!? I thought I signed up for some devotions here!"

Any journey worth taking will involve some challenges. But you're up to it. You're serious about this, or you wouldn't be here now. God says we are to observe His Word, to be daily meditating on it. Put feet to your faith. Make a commitment to start today, and memorize one new Scripture verse weekly for the next ten weeks. For the twelfth week, review the ten verses and consider making this a regular practice in your life. Choose verses that have real meaning to you so it is a part of your relationship with God, not simply another "chore." If you have difficulty with memorization, this is a real opportunity to draw near to God and enlist the help of the Holy Spirit and maybe a friend or prayer partner to have fun with it.

By filling your mind daily with the Word of God, you will choke out the cares of the world and be saturated with His Spirit.

In your journal, make a note of the verse you'll memorize and your plan for doing it.

_____

_____

_____

_____

_____

_____

_____

PROTECT YOUR HUNGER

"A satisfied soul loathes the honeycomb, but to a hungry soul every bitter thing is sweet."
Proverbs 27:7

KEY STATEMENT: Too often we are indifferent in our desire for the things of God.

Most do not despise His presence, but compared to the hungry man, they are offhanded toward the feast God has laid out before them.

Ask yourself these questions:
- Am I indifferent to the things of God?
- Have I forgotten my first love?
- Do I still have compassion for the lost souls of the world?
- Do I pray for people and the nations daily, or at least regularly?
- Does my soul still pant for Him?
- Do I read the Bible daily?
- Am I hungry for the things of God?

After careful examination of these questions, spend time in prayer before the Lord. Pray for the nations and others. Make a decision to rekindle your love for the Lord. Journal below what the Lord speaks to your heart, including names of those you prayed for.

_____

_____

_____

_____

_____

_____

_____

_____

_____

_____

_____

_____

_____

_____

_____

PROTECT YOUR HUNGER

"Here I am! I stand at the door and knock. If anyone hears my voice and opens the door, I will come in and eat with him, and he with me."
Revelation 3:20, NIV

KEY STATEMENT: There is a remedy for an indifferent heart.

How often do you go out and eat a meal at a restaurant with your family or friends to satisfy your physical needs? _____ We feed our bodies daily, and often dine with family or friends on a weekly basis.

When was the last time you set aside time to sup with the Lord and hear from Him so that your spiritual needs were met? _____

God sent Moses to the backside of the desert away from all distractions so that he might be able to hear clearly the voice of the Lord speaking to him. In his single encounter with the burning bush, God obtained Moses' attention, and Moses never became distracted again. He lived a *life* of intimacy with the Lord.

Journal below what the Lord speaks to you about these things as you meditate on His Word and worship Him.

_____

_____

_____

_____

_____

_____

_____

_____

_____

_____

Spiritual neglect will cause you to have an apathetic heart. If you truly desire a relationship of intimacy with the Lord, then make the decision to live a LIFETIME of intimacy with Him! PLAN an appointment with Him daily so that you may open your heart before Him and hear what He has to say. God desires your attention. You can't afford not to keep your daily time with God.

PROTECT YOUR HUNGER

"Or do you not know that your body is the temple of the Holy Spirit who is in you, whom you have from God, and you are not your own? For you were bought at a price; therefore glorify God in your body and in your spirit, which are God's."

I Corinthians 6:19–20

KEY STATEMENT: Hunger is the key element to whether or not we pursue intimacy with God.

The dictionary defines hunger as *"having an urgent need or eager desire."*

Does this describe your hunger for your relationship with God?

[ ] **Yes**   [ ] **No**   [ ] **Sometimes**

Cravings for the wrong foods can kill the success of a diet. The same applies to spiritual things. Craving the wrong things can destroy our spiritual diet. What are some strong cravings that could be weeded out of your life?

_____

_____

A craving is a strong desire. A strong desire in your life could be coffee, a certain television show, finances, sports, approval of others, etc.

We need to have a steady diet of God's Word and times with Him. In doing this, we will have intimate times of prayer and conversations with the Lord, *and spiritual things will come naturally because we have made the presence of the Lord an integral part of our lives.* Remember, this journey is about a *life(time)* of intimacy with God.

 Meditate on this and record what the Lord shares with you. When you draw near to Him, be ready for Him to draw near to you, too. You may be surprised at what He does here. Be open to His loving correction. He wants to help you weed out any sinful cravings or poor habits. He can empower you to add some good habits to your life. Be open to both!

_____

_____

_____

_____

_____

_____

_____

We are in control of our appetite, not God.

PROTECT YOUR HUNGER

Week 2 Day 12

"The thief does not come except to steal, and to kill, and to destroy. I have come that they may have life, and that they may have it more abundantly."
John 10:10

KEY STATEMENT: Are you too busy?

Let's take time today to look at Mary and Martha in the Bible. **Read Luke 10:38–42. It says in verse 40,** *"But Martha was distracted with much serving..."*

In today's world it is extremely easy to keep oneself busy and distracted. We have unlimited access to information from all around the world through use of the Internet. Hollywood produces more movies than we could ever hope to watch. Tomorrow there will be a better car produced, a newer version of the computer program that you just purchased, a camera that can focus on objects as clearly as a bird can see, and the list is endless.

We often have taken our lives to unhealthy extremes. No matter how much we see or do, we will never be satisfied. Our lives will continue to seem tiresome, unfulfilling, and uncontrollable without an intimate life of fellowship with our Father God.

Many things can have a place in our lives, but it is easy to see how Satan has used these avenues to steal our money and time, and to kill and destroy our relationship with not only our families, but also more importantly, our intimate relationship with God. Jesus said that we are worried and troubled with many things. He also said, *"But one thing is needed, and Mary has chosen that good part, which will not be taken away from her"* (v. 42).

Take time today to examine your life. Write down what your typical day and/or week consists of.

_____

_____

_____

_____

_____

_____

_____

Make time for the Lover of your soul. Honestly, are there things that may be eliminated from your daily, weekly, or yearly schedule to cause you to be less busy?

If so, what are they? _____

How can you follow through on this?_____

PROTECT YOUR HUNGER

Week 2 Day 13

"And Jesus answered and said to her, 'Martha, Martha, you are worried and troubled about many things. But one thing is needed, and Mary has chosen that good part, which will not be taken from her.'"
Luke 10:41–42

KEY STATEMENT: Are you doing what is needful?

Many well-meaning believers have replaced their time with God with busy Christian lifestyles. This includes what can be the deceptive and continuous labor of ministry.

Is your life scheduled with an overabundance of church activities that keep you from spending quiet time with God? [ ] **Yes**   [ ] **No**   [ ] **Don't know**

Yes, you should be involved with your local church. Find what your gifts and talents are, and find ways to serve God (for example: going to church weekly without excuses, serving as a greeter or an usher, helping with vacation Bible school, making food for others, etc.). But let's not confuse the issue: God-ordained ministry is a RESULT of our intimate relations with Him, as opposed to the mistaken notion that busyness "FOR" God somehow equates to intimacy WITH God.

Jesus did not necessarily say that what Martha was doing was not needful; He said Mary had chosen the good part (spiritual time with Him), and that would not be taken from her. We must balance our time and not get caught up in busyness for its own sake.

Remember yesterday's devotion. Have you scheduled ample time with God in your life?
_____ (Remember, your time with God is the very wellspring of your life.)

If not, what it is that is hindering you?

_____

_____

What are you willing to do to change this? _____

_____

Do you need to reassess your involvement in your church? More? Less? Is it the right kind of involvement for the right reasons?

Journal Notes:

_____

_____

_____

_____

He is always faithful to speak as we come into His presence.

PROTECT YOUR HUNGER

"Keep your heart with all diligence, for out of it spring the issues of life."
Proverbs 4:23

KEY STATEMENT: The most valuable possession on earth—your heart.

We have banks and vaults to protect "things" that will one day pass away. They seem to have a huge value since thousands of dollars are spent to guard them and keep them safe. These men are wise because they guard what they value the most, even though it is worldly. Mankind has placed a high value on these things, but God says that there is something else of much more value—your heart!

Believers become careless because they fail to guard their hearts from worldly lusts by allowing things that are harmful to enter their spirits. We do this because we become complacent and our hearts become seared. What we would not say or do when we first accepted Jesus in our heart, we allow now. We let down our guard and neglect the filter of the Holy Spirit. We must guard our heart with all diligence!

What worldly things might you be full of that steal your hunger and desire? What has replaced the spiritual issues of life from God's Word? What may have replaced your longing to be satisfied by Him alone? Let the Holy Spirit search your heart here. Some examples could be the intense desire for a spouse or children, a career, or even a college degree. Perhaps you have an addiction. It can be surprising what things we allow to quench our passion for God. Let Him move deeply in you right now as you worship.

_____

_____

_____

Review days eight to fourteen. Prayerfully summarize your week.

_____

Feet to your Faith: List what actions you will take to help protect your heart, and let His goodness satisfy you. Don't set some lofty goal(s), but do rely on the Holy Spirit to help you.

_____

_____

Keep your heart hungry, and let His goodness satisfy you. It is drawing near to Him that will cause Him to fulfill His promise of drawing near to you.

It's a promise from Him to you: "For He satisfies the longing soul, and fills the hungry soul with goodness."
Psalms 107:9

PROTECT YOUR HUNGER

Additional Notes

PASSION FOR HIS PRESENCE

Week 3 Day 15

"Now the LORD had said to Abram: 'Get out of your country, from your family and from your father's house, to a land that I will show you. I will make you a great nation; I will bless you and make your name great; and you shall be a blessing. I will bless those who bless you, and I will curse him who curses you; and in you all the families of the earth shall be blessed.'"

Genesis 12:1–3

KEY STATEMENT: "A journey of a thousand miles must begin with a single step."

-Chinese Proverb

If you were going on a journey, a vacation or a trip, paint a picture in your mind of the details of it.

Where would you go?_____

Why did you choose this place?_____

What would you do while you were there? List sites you would visit (museums, parks); cities you would tour; places you would eat, etc._____

_____

What kind of people would you meet?_____

What would you talk about?_____

_____

What lasting impressions would you want to journal so that you could look back at what you wrote to remember the trip?_____

_____

That exercise tends to be a bit exciting—planning, imagining, almost playing. Now think of God speaking to Abraham. What must have been going through Abraham's mind? This was no vacation or imaginary trip. He had to leave his country, his father's house, his family—everything. And go to…well, he wasn't even sure of where, how, or what. This was actually God's will! You may be feeling a bit like that now on this spiritual journey. But rest assured; though you may not know exactly where you are headed, God has a plan for you. Worship Jesus and let Him minister to you.

Be encouraged by the Holy Spirit, and write some lasting impressions from this REAL journey you are living right now!

_____

_____

_____

_____

PASSION FOR HIS PRESENCE

Week 3 Day 16

"So Abram departed as the LORD had spoken to him…
Genesis 12:4

KEY STATEMENT: Like Abraham, you are on a journey.

Abram did not plan his destination of where he wanted to go and what he wanted to see along the way. Abram's story is actually a spiritual odyssey—a journey like what you are doing on this journey to His heart.

God spoke to Abram and told him to *"get out of your country…to a land that I will show you."* It was by faith that he obeyed God, left the land of Haran, and journeyed to the place that he knew not of. God is asking you to take that same journey of faith.

Journey is an action word; it implies movement. God asks you to put feet to your faith. He wants you to be willing and obedient so that He can bless you and you can meet the needs of those whom He has placed along your path.

What is God asking you to do to meet the needs of others?_____

_____

_____

Write how you can put **feet to your faith** and meet these needs:

_____

_____

_____

Now write the date that you will do this:_____

_____

As you worship the Lord today, what is He saying about your journey?

_____

_____

_____

Write your memory verse for this week: _____

_____

_____

My heart has heard you say, "Come and talk with me." And my heart
responds, "LORD, I am coming."
Psalms 27:8, NLT

PASSION FOR HIS PRESENCE

*"Blessed (happy, fortunate, to be envied) are those who dwell in Your house and Your presence;
they will be singing your praises all the day long. Selah [pause, and calmly think of that]!"*
Psalms 84:4, AMP

KEY STATEMENT: We were created to dwell with God in reality, not just theory.

If this journey were a cold and impersonal study in theological theory, it would probably get old fast. Either that, or you would settle for a mental relationship with God. Doctrine is always very important, but it's hard to have relationship with a theory or a debate topic.

Abraham, Moses, David, Paul—these men would not make a move if God's presence did not go with them—and so should it be today with us in the church.

Going to church, going to school or the office, time with your family and friends:
* Have you gotten used to going through your daily life on your own, or do you rely on God?
* Do you need who He is in your life in all you do?
* Have you developed the habit of needing God's Word and the power of the Holy Spirit to succeed in your daily life?

In today's worship and journaling time, ask yourself those questions. Go beyond theory. Fall on your knees and seek God Himself today. Learn to practice the presence of the Lord in all you do.

_____
_____
_____
_____
_____
_____
_____
_____
_____
_____
_____
_____
_____
_____
_____

PASSION FOR HIS PRESENCE

Week 3 Day 18

"If Your presence does not go with us, do not bring us up from here."
Exodus 33:15

KEY STATEMENT: The spoken Word is heard when we are in His presence.

When God spoke to Moses to lead His people, Moses was in the desert—a dry and barren place. A place of hardship, void of comfort and pleasures. There were no gardens, homes, rivers, fields, fruit trees, shopping malls, or entertainment. There was no abundance to be found, yet Moses would not leave that place unless God went with him.

Moses knew what it was to live in "luxury" because he was raised in the home of Pharaoh. But he chose to leave behind the finest things and all the comforts that the world had to offer. He also chose to resign and give up the highest status a person could achieve.

Why? Moses left it all behind because he had encountered the God of the universe. He knew that there was more to life than just earthly pleasures. Moses realized that he needed the presence of the Lord. And this is what we need too.

In order to be successful on your journey to His heart, you must have His presence. This is when God reveals Himself to our spirits, and when our mind and senses become aware of His nearness as well.

Besides Abraham and Moses, list others from the Bible that God manifested His presence to: _____

_____

List times when God has manifested Himself in your life: _____

_____

_____

In today's time with God, be like our examples in the Bible. Humble yourself before God. Tell Him you won't live and move anymore without His presence, and ask the Holy Spirit to speak to you about this very thing.

_____

_____

_____

_____

_____

_____

PASSION FOR HIS PRESENCE

"I long, yes, faint with longing to be able to enter your courtyard and come near to the Living God."
Psalms 84:2, TLB

KEY STATEMENT: We were all created for God, and none of us will ever find true fulfillment outside of knowing Him and walking in His presence.

The children of Israel followed Moses into the wilderness. They believed in the same God as Moses, yet they each had a different relationship with God. In the desert, Moses experienced God's manifest presence. He met with God on the mountain; God gave him the Ten Commandments, and his face shone with the glory of the Lord. Yet the people of Israel were not interested in this type of relationship. They wanted Moses to speak to the Lord for them, and then Moses was to tell them what God had said. The people complained and wanted their needs fulfilled. Moses was content and longed to be in the presence of God.

What a stark contrast. Moses sought God's presence while Israel sought God's manifestations. We need to make sure that we are seeking God Himself and not the manifestations. We must realize that our deepest longings will never be satisfied until we follow after a true life of intimacy with Him.

Do you have a void or a sense of needing more in your life? [ ] Yes [ ] No

Have you tried to fill it with activities, movies, clothes, friends, or material things?
[ ] Yes [ ] No

God's desire through salvation was to draw you near to Him so the two of you could walk in the beauty of His presence. Is this your heart's desire?

In today's time with God, meditate on the contrast between Moses and the children of Israel. Speak to God of His beauty, holiness, and love. In Him you live and move and have your very being. Now let loose and pray that way.

_____

_____

_____

_____

_____

_____

_____

PASSION FOR HIS PRESENCE

Week 3 Day 20

"Declare His glory among the nations, His wonders among all peoples."
Psalms 96:3

"The heavens declare His righteousness, and all the peoples see His glory."
Psalms 97:6

KEY STATEMENT: "Please, show me Your glory."

How would you describe God's glory? _____

_____

Strong's Bible Dictionary describes glory as "the weight of something, but only figuratively in a good sense." It also means beauty, splendor, and magnificence.

We can observe many magnificent and beautiful things that the Lord has created. Everyday you can see there is no end to God's creation.

Satan uses the world to skew and cloud our vision of true glory. Advertisers, movies, and commercials portray that beauty and glory can be found in looks, money, and possessions. The world tells you that if you possess any of these, they are worthy of glorification.

God's glory is different from that of the world. Why do you need God's glory?

_____

_____

_____

When Moses asked to see God's glory, God responded by saying, *"I will make all My goodness pass before you, and I will proclaim the name of the LORD before you"* (Exod. 33:19). The Hebrew word for goodness is "good in the widest sense." One reason we need God's glory is because it is how He shows us His goodness.

Where was the glory of the Lord found dwelling in the Old Testament?
[ ] Heaven [ ] The priests [ ] The Tabernacle

Where can you find the glory of the Lord dwelling today?
[ ] Heaven [ ] The pastor [ ] Us

In today's time of worship, ask God, "Show me your glory both in me and through me to others."

_____

_____

_____

_____

Answer: The Tabernacle, Us

22

PASSION FOR HIS PRESENCE

Week 3 Day 21

"You don't need to go to heaven (to find Christ and bring him down to help you)."
Romans 10:6, NLT

"I will pray the Father, and He will give you another Helper, that He may abide with you forever—the Spirit of truth, whom the world cannot receive, because it neither sees Him nor knows Him; but you know Him, for He dwells with you and will be in you."
John 14:16–17

KEY STATEMENT: The Holy Spirit lives in you!

When you think of God and picture Him in your mind, where do you see Him?
[ ] On the cross [ ] In heaven [ ] In church [ ] In your heart

God no longer dwells in a tent or a temple like in the Old Testament. Now He has made His abode in our hearts!

• Why don't more people want to enjoy an intimate relationship with Him?
• What is it that hinders us?
• Why do we still struggle in our own strength instead of trusting and relying on Him?
• Why are so many people dissatisfied with life?

These are valid questions, and you will discover more as you go. However, the answer today is as straightforward as it ever has been. Jesus said to believers that He stands at the door and knocks. James 4:8 in The Message translation says this: "Say a quiet yes to God and he'll be there in no time." That's really your devotional and journaling time for today and every day.

_____

_____

_____

_____

_____

_____

_____

_____

_____

_____

_____

Answer: In your heart

Additional Notes

THE FRIENDS OF GOD

Week 4 Day 22

*"God is greatly to be feared in the assembly of the saints, and to be held in reverence
by all those around Him."*
Psalms 89:7

KEY STATEMENT: You will find the Lord where He is held in the utmost of
respect and reverence.

God is the holy and great King and as such is to be revered. Therefore you cannot speak of
"drawing near" without first understanding "holy fear." The way to approach Him is by
the path bordered by both holy love and holy fear.

To "fear" God means to esteem, honor, and hold Him in highest regard, as well as to
venerate, stand in awe, and reverence Him. It is to tremble with the greatest respect for
Him, His presence, and His commands.

The fear of the Lord begins in the heart and then manifests itself in your outward
actions. Drawing near always begins in a heart that fears and loves God more than
anyone or anything else. It is not just outward actions, but the heart's motive.

*"These people draw near with their mouths and honor Me with their lips, but have removed their
hearts far from Me, and their fear toward Me is taught by the commandment of men."*
Isaiah 29:13

*Spend time with the Lord, searching the thoughts and intents of your heart. Does what you say and
do daily honor Him? Your outward actions should reveal a heart that holds God in reverence. Tell
Him how much you love and fear Him, for if you love Him, you will keep His commands.*

_____

_____

_____

_____

_____

_____

_____

_____

_____

_____

_____

THE FRIENDS OF GOD

Week 4 Day 23

"Nadab and Abihu, the sons of Aaron, each took his censer and put fire in it, put incense on it, and offered profane fire before the LORD, which He had not commanded them. So fire went out from the LORD and devoured them, and they died before the LORD."

Leviticus 10:1–2

KEY STATEMENT: The root of sin is the lack of the fear of the Lord.

Nadab and Abihu offered profane fire before the Lord. Profane is defined as "showing disrespect or contempt for sacred things; irreverent." It means to treat what God calls holy or sacred as if it were common. These two men were set apart and trained to minister to the Lord. Yet they approached the presence of the Lord with an irreverent incense offering, and they died before the Lord.

Why did this happen?
- They filled the censers with the fire and incense of their own choosing and not the one God had chosen.
- They were careless with what was holy, and this led to their disobedience.
- Nadab and Abihu were instantly judged for their irreverence and met with immediate death.
- They sinned by approaching a holy God as though He were common.
- They had become too familiar with His presence and took it for granted.

As you draw near to God today, ask Him what you can learn about your own life from Nadab and Abihu. Are you casual or reverent? Expectant or full of doubt? Journal today what the Lord tells you about how to properly approach Him in every area of your life—personal prayer time, work and family, and, of course, church.

_____

_____

_____

_____

_____

_____

_____

_____

_____

_____

*Write your memory verse for this week:*_____

_____

THE FRIENDS OF GOD

Week 4 Day 24

"For God has not given us a spirit of fear, but of power and of love and of a sound mind."
2 Timothy 1:7

*"Let us therefore come boldly to the throne of grace, that we may obtain mercy
and find grace to help in time of need."*
Hebrews 4:16

KEY STATEMENT: We must fear God, not be afraid of God.

Reverence and humility before God, this healthy fear is not what keeps us *from Him* but is actually *the very doorway* into His presence. It is the contrite heart with which God fellowships.

When you come before God in today's time with Him, realize that as you bow down He actually lifts you up. It is by grace we are saved, and you are about to enter into an audience with the King, who knew you before you were born, named you from eternity past and future, and calls you to a romance with Him! **Live this life of intimacy with God with all the passion and the heart of a servant whom the King actually desires to call "friend."**

There are many Christians who call Jesus their Savior and love Him, but they don't fear Him as their supreme Lord. They love an image of "Jesus" they have created from their own imagination and understanding of the Scriptures. They worship a distorted image of who God really is.

We tend to be scared of God because we have something to hide or because we don't know of the love and work of Jesus on our behalf that enables us to come into God's presence boldly. The fear of God is not about being afraid; it's about the majesty of God. If He is your Lord, you will keep His commandments. You will tremble at His Word. You will love what He loves and hate what He hates. You will worship and serve Him even when you don't see the benefit of it. Those who fear Him are no longer servants but friends.

THE FRIENDS OF GOD

Week 4 Day 25

"I went slowly towards them. When I came within eight or ten feet of her, I looked solemnly at her. She observed it, and was quite overcome, and sunk down, and burst into tears. The impression caught almost like powder, and in a few moments nearly all in the room were in tears. This feeling spread through the factory. The owner of the establishment was present, and seeing the state of things, he said to the superintendent, 'Stop the mill, and let the people attend to religion; for it is more important that our souls should be saved than that this factory run.'

We did so, and a more powerful meeting I scarcely ever attended. It went on with great power. The building was large, and had many people in it, from the garret to the cellar. The revival went through the mill with astonishing power, and in the course of a few days nearly all in the mill were hopefully converted." [2]

(An account from the autobiography of Charles Finney as he was invited to tour a factory during year 1825)

"Now it was so, when Moses came down from Mount Sinai...that Moses did not know that the skin of his face shone while he talked with Him. So when Aaron and all the children of Israel saw Moses, behold, the skin of his face shone, and they were afraid to come near him."
Exodus 34:29–30

KEY STATEMENT: The secret of the Lord is with those who fear Him.

Charles Finney was a New York lawyer who became one of history's great evangelists. Moses left a prestigious life to obey God and walk with Him in His presence. What was their secret? What did they know that we don't? What gave them the ability to simply stand in the presence of men and bring the very presence of God? On this journey *you have found the answer!* The secret of the Lord is with those who fear Him. Finney spent hours seeking God; Moses did the same.

You cannot afford NOT to know the secrets of the Lord for your life and the lives of those around you! Don't be one of the masses that wonder why God seems special to others and is always speaking to and blessing others. YOU draw near; YOU press in. Fear Him, adore Him, and He will share His secrets with you!

_____

_____

_____

_____

_____

_____

_____

_____

THE FRIENDS OF GOD

"However, when He, the Spirit of truth, has come, He will guide you into all truth; for He will not speak on His own authority, but whatever He hears He will speak; and He will tell you things to come."
John 16:13

"I fell on my knees with my arms over the seat in front of me and the tears flowed freely. I cried, 'Bend me! Bend me! Bend me! Bend us!'…Perspiration poured down my face and tears streamed quickly until I thought that the blood came out. Now a great burden came upon me for the salvation of lost souls." [3]
The words of young Evan Roberts, September 29, 1904

KEY STATEMENT: Are you clueless or clued in?

According to the Bible, both Abraham and Lot were righteous men. God told Abraham of His intentions to destroy the cities where Lot lived. The Lord even approached Abraham to discuss the situation, and He valued and heeded his input. Lot, on the other hand, had no idea that he was hours away from the destruction of his home.

For thirteen years, Evan Roberts was always in prayer meetings, believing that the Holy Spirit would come and bring revival to his nation. Within a month of the prayer above he declared to family members and his pastor "there will be a great change in Lougher in less than a fortnight. We are going to have the greatest revival that Wales has ever seen." Within a year, more than 100,000 people were in the midst of the Welsh Revival, led by Evan Roberts.

How did he know? How did Abraham know? Why them? You are finding some great things on this journey, and here is your answer. Don't forget Abraham by this time had spent years practicing the habit of the presence of the Lord and obedience to Him. Evan Roberts was always at those prayer meetings—thirteen years—crying out to God to save his nation.

Do you want God? Go for Him. Change your habits, let loose the cares of this world, and get clued in. Fall on your knees; cry out, "Bend me, O God!" Take it a step further: "Break me, O God!" Empty yourself of self and get filled with God. Draw near to Him, and see what He tells you as you do so!

_____

_____

_____

_____

_____

_____

_____

THE FRIENDS OF GOD

Week 4 Day 27

"You are My friends if you do whatever I command you."
John 15:14

KEY STATEMENT: We must be mindful of whom we worship.

In today's media-driven culture, the church falls into the trap of nearly worshiping any dignitary, celebrity, person, or thing the media anoint as worthy. We feel we know these famous people. We feel close with them and that they are worthy of respect and our attentions because of their fame, position, and/or attainments.

Famous people want us to feel very close to them. They want us to believe that they care about us, love us, respect us, and that they feel as close to us as we feel close to them. (This is one of the ways they increase their fame and fortune.) *However, just try being intimate with Madonna, Michael Jordan, or the president of the United States*—and you will quickly find they do NOT want your intimacy. What's more, you could find yourself imprisoned if you try to get too close to them!

Yet God Almighty is immeasurably closer to us than any famous person, and He does desire our intimacy! Furthermore, of course, God will do much more in and for our lives than even the most revered public figure.

Jesus said, "If you love Me, you will keep My commandments." That certainly is very different from the media who say, "If you love me, you will buy my stuff." It may be OK to be a fan of a fine musician, and certainly it is right to respect a dignitary, but we need to keep our priorities straight. There is only one King of kings and Lord of lords and God of all creation.

Today think on these things, and worship the One who is truly worthy.

_____

_____

_____

_____

_____

_____

_____

_____

_____

_____

_____

_____

THE FRIENDS OF GOD

"No longer do I call you servants, for a servant does not know what his master is doing; but I have called you friends, for all things that I heard from My Father I have made known to you."
John 15:15

KEY STATEMENT: The fear of the Lord is the key to intimacy with God and the foundation for life.

Western culture seems to be obsessed with the cult of personality. Rock stars, movie stars, politicians, and sports and business figures—we want to be like them. We desire their minds, bodies, power, abilities, fortunes, and more.

Why do we emulate them? The list of people we want to be "just like" is endless. The sad irony is, of course, that we will never be just like Donald Trump, Nelson Mandela, Tiger Woods, Nancy Reagan, or Billy Graham. We can covet being like them all we want, but it's not going to happen, even if we get close to them.

Jesus is the one famous personality that WANTS us near Him. He *desires* us to want to be like Him! And the beauty of this is that God is the most famed, most beautiful, most powerful, most influential, and most able "person" there ever was! He is the one "ultra-famous personality" who actually invites you—gives you 24/7 (24 hours per day, 7 days per week) access—to His very inner chamber! He wants you to draw near to Him so you may be transformed into His very image and become the person you should be!

Let's not build our lives on the false foundation that the world creates for us. Build it on the sure foundation—Jesus.

Think about what you have gone through so far on this journey, and make your notes of the things God has spoken to you. He no longer desires to call you servant. He desires to be your "friend."

_____

_____

_____

_____

_____

_____

_____

_____

_____

_____

THE FRIENDS OF GOD

Additional Notes

WHAT HINDERS TRUE INTIMACY

Week 5 Day 29

"For there is one God and one Mediator between God and men, the Man Christ Jesus."
I Timothy 2:5

"But now He has obtained a more excellent ministry, inasmuch as He is also Mediator of a better covenant, which was established on better promises."
Hebrews 8:6

KEY STATEMENT: Don't draw back; draw near.

When Moses brought the people of God to meet God at Sinai, the people stood afar off while Moses drew near. God then called Moses and Aaron up the mountain as mediators between Himself and the people. Moses ends up on the mountain in the presence of God, and the next thing we know Aaron is back down among the people.

Today God is calling you "to the mountain." He desires you to come into His presence. Better yet is the fact that you can come *directly* into His presence through the blood of Jesus.

Are you like a Moses who will boldly and obediently climb the mountain, or an Aaron who begins the ascent but seemingly went back to camp? Worse yet, are you among those who stand afar off, never entering His presence?

You are well into your adventure. God is wooing you right now. Imagine you are Aaron and are part way up the mountain, obedient on your journey to come up where God has commanded you. But you have a decision to make.

Now is not the time to turn back. Make your prayer time today really count. Don't draw back; draw near and journal the encouraging words the Holy Spirit will speak to help you finish the race you've begun!

_____

_____

_____

_____

_____

_____

_____

_____

_____

WHAT HINDERS TRUE INTIMACY

"The eyes of the LORD are in every place, keeping watch on the evil and the good."
Proverbs 15:3

KEY STATEMENT: Pride keeps you from admitting you are religious, and religion covers the pride with its spiritual mannerisms.

That's a pretty heavy thought, so take time to read it again. Adam's son Cain, attempting to serve God, brought an offering of the fruit of the ground. Yet God had clothed Adam and Eve in the skins of an animal sacrifice. When God told Cain his sacrifice was unacceptable, Cain was very angry with God.

Uzziah became king when he was sixteen years old. He sought God and prospered until he became strong. Then he, like Cain, presumed to bring God an unacceptable sacrifice. When he was confronted, he too became furious.

Although outwardly appearing to seek intimacy with God, these two men in reality further distanced themselves from the One they sought to worship. They looked spiritual, but when they were confronted with truth, their pride rose up and revealed itself.

Could you be hearing the voice of your own imaginings and not Jesus at all in some areas? Have you sought intimacy only to find self-deception? Do not assume it can't happen to you; rather let the Holy Spirit lead you deeper in your walk with Him as you spend time with Him today!

_____

_____

_____

_____

_____

_____

_____

_____

_____

_____

Write this week's memory verse here: _____

_____

_____

WHAT HINDERS TRUE INTIMACY

Week 5 Day 31

"And the word of the LORD came to me, saying, 'Son of man, these men have set up their idols in their hearts, and put before them that which causes them to stumble into iniquity. Should I let Myself be inquired of at all by them?'"
Ezekiel 14:2–3

KEY STATEMENT: When we fear God, we should come to Him with a neutral heart, ready to hear His words of instruction or correction.

Approaching the Lord with strong desires that are not in line with His will, when He has made His will known to us, can prove to be a most unwise and dangerous thing. This can lead us to the next level of deception, which is even more serious. This next level of deception is when God Himself will actually give us, or allow us to have, what we want.

Even more sobering is when God considers not even letting Himself listen to us (v. 3)! When we set up idols in our hearts that are at enmity with God, we actually may construct barriers to God's hearing us.

Take time to examine your heart. Idols are not only statue images found in people's yards or homes, nor is idolatry only when someone calls on the name of a foreign god. The idolatry God was speaking of was found in their hearts. It is possible to come to God so filled with our own desires that we reduce Him to an image that will give us what we desire.

Are your desires God's desires? When you meet with God today, check your heart and say, "Lord, what is it You want me to do?" If you can't separate your desires from God's, ask the Holy Spirit to make your heart neutral, rooting out any desire for personal gain.

Journal below the ways in which God divides your desires from His true desires:

_____

_____

_____

_____

_____

_____

_____

_____

_____

_____

WHAT HINDERS TRUE INTIMACY

Week 5 Day 32

"Let your conduct be without covetousness; be content with such things as you have. For He Himself has said, 'I will never leave you nor forsake you.'"
Hebrews 13:5

"I feel it is far better to begin (the day) with God—to see His face first, to get my soul near Him before it is near another." [4]
Robert Murray McCheyne

"I urge upon you communion with Christ, a growing communion. There are curtains to be drawn aside in Christ that we never saw, and new foldings of love in Him. Therefore dig deep, and sweat and labor and take pains for Him, and set by as much time in the day for Him as you can. He will be won in the labor." [5]
Samuel Rutherford

KEY STATEMENT: Our life must be one of contentment, not covetousness.

Covetousness is the desire for gain. This does not limit covetousness to the desire for money. This encompasses possessions, position, comfort, acceptance, pleasure, power, sexual lust, and so on. Covetousness is the state we find ourselves in when we're not content.

Discontentment causes us to resist God's plan and processes in our lives. That is why we are to "let our conduct be without covetousness." Yes—our culture tells us we need everything but God to be content. Yes—politics and our educational system send a confusing message about God. But these are neither excuses nor good reasons for our own conduct to be weakened through the covetousness, the constant desire for more, that pervades our society. The simple fact is we have God. If we think we need more, we are in error.

Ask God to breathe into you that life which is content with Him alone. Ask God to help you dig deep in prayer so you find new foldings of love in Him. Let the romance and passion, the very food of the Bread of Life, be your contentment today and every day.

_____

_____

_____

_____

_____

_____

_____

_____

_____

WHAT HINDERS TRUE INTIMACY

Week 5 Day 33

"You shall not make idols for yourselves."
Leviticus 26:1

"But each one is tempted when he is drawn away by his own desires and enticed."
James 1:14

KEY STATEMENT: Idols are a poor substitute for the provision and joy of God Himself.

Regardless of what form they take (possessions, position, pleasures, etc.), idols serve as a source of happiness, peace, or provision. An idol is something we make and put before God. It is anything we love, like, trust, desire, or give our attention to more than the Lord. An idol is what you tend to draw your strength from or give your strength to.

The people of God are not supposed to have idols. Idolatry is sin. Our Father God, who always knows and does what is best for us, is to be our source of happiness, peace, and provision. It is Jesus we are to love, trust, desire, and give our attention to. The Holy Spirit is the one from whom we draw our strength.

Leviticus makes it clear that we make our own idols. James says we are drawn away by our own desires. Satan may entice us, but he tempts us with the things we desire.

At times growing up is a challenge. But boy—isn't it great when you finally get the keys to the car! And so it is with God. If we are to be mature believers, real disciples of Jesus, we have to grow in grace and truth in the Word of God. Facing, then forsaking, our own idolatry is definitely a part of that. Rejoice! Count it all joy as you enter the courts of God and He calls you higher!

Ask the Holy Spirit to show you any and all idolatry in your life. Repent and seek God's restoration. Journal what happens today. Let God be your source!

_____

_____

_____

_____

_____

_____

_____

_____

_____

WHAT HINDERS TRUE INTIMACY

"Be energetic in your life of salvation, reverent and sensitive before God. That energy is God's energy, an energy deep within you, God Himself willing and working at what will give him the most pleasure."
Philippians 2:12–13, The Message, emphasis added

*"Wherefore, my beloved, as ye have always obeyed, not as in my presence only, but now much more in my absence, work out your own salvation with fear and trembling.
For it is God which worketh in you both to will and to do of his good pleasure."*
Philippians 2:12–13, KJV

"Submit yourselves therefore to God. Resist the devil, and he will flee from you."
James 4:7, KJV

*"I judge that my prayer is more than the devil himself; if it were otherwise,
I would have fared differently long before this."*
"If I should neglect prayer but a single day, I should lose a great deal of the fire of faith." [6]
Martin Luther

KEY STATEMENT: Resisting the devil in prayer and with our lifestyle is part of our journey.

The things you've been delving into on this journey are about working out your salvation. The fear of God and trembling at His Word are exactly how this is done. The energy to do this comes from God Himself as He wills and works in your life as you seek Him.

For today's time, look back at your desires, idolatry, and the way in which you approach God. Take a lesson from the great Martin Luther. Today is going to be great. Name the temptations, any wrong desires, and anything else that proceeds from the pit of hell to entice you away from God's heart.

Right now, joyfully and strongly, with the Word of God, resist the devil, and he will flee from you.

_____

_____

_____

_____

_____

_____

_____

_____

_____

_____

_____

_____

WHAT HINDERS TRUE INTIMACY

"Him we preach and proclaim, warning and admonishing everyone and instructing everyone in all wisdom (comprehensive insight into the ways and purposes of God), that we may present every person mature (full-grown, fully initiated, complete and perfect) in Christ (the Anointed One)."
Colossians 1:28, AMP

"Therefore let him who thinks he stands take heed lest he fall."
I Corinthians 10:12

KEY STATEMENT: God Himself is our benchmark of truth.

This has been an intense week in your journey: rooting out and pulling down, building up and strengthening by the Word of God. The very truth that brings joy can also be sobering. Warnings at first glance might not appear positive, yet in the end they are life-saving and produce fruit when heeded. It is so important that we not fall into the trap of being one-sided in our gospel—always emphasizing the positive, or even the negative.

Balance is key, and our level, measuring stick, or plumb line—however you want to put it—is the Word of God. The Holy Spirit is our divine benchmark of truth.

Journal today some things you have learned along the journey, including how your image of God has changed. What have you learned from the Scriptures and teachings each day that is bearing fruit in your life? Finish by asking God to continue meaningful change in your life and then praising Him by faith that He will complete what He started.

_____

_____

_____

_____

_____

_____

_____

_____

_____

_____

WHAT HINDERS TRUE INTIMACY

Additional Notes

_____

_____

_____

_____

_____

_____

_____

_____

_____

_____

_____

_____

_____

_____

_____

_____

_____

_____

_____

_____

_____

_____

_____

_____

_____

_____

_____

_____

TRUE WORSHIP

"This is the history of Noah and his family. Noah was a righteous man, the only blameless man living on earth at the time. He consistently followed God's will and enjoyed a close relationship with him."
Genesis 6:9, NLT

"He [God] raised up for them David as king, to whom also He gave testimony and said, 'I have found David the son of Jesse, a man after My own heart, who will do all My will.'"
Acts 13:22

KEY STATEMENT: A religious spirit is one who uses God's Word to execute his own desire.

Deception knocks at the door of those who lack the fear of the Lord in their lives. On the other hand, intimacy knocks at the door of those who continually draw near to the Lord in holy fear. Obedience and a heart to fulfill His will are characteristics found in the lives of those who walk with God.

- Enoch's testimony was that he walked in intimate communion with the Lord and pleased Him because of his righteous obedience.

- Noah's testimony was that he pleased the Lord because he consistently followed God's will and enjoyed a close relationship with Him.

- David's testimony was that he pleased the Lord because he was a man after God's own heart.

True worship and the fear of the Lord are when you obey and fulfill all His will. In your prayer time today, ask the Lord to show you how you can carry out His wishes and desires as if they were your own.

_____

_____

_____

_____

_____

_____

_____

_____

_____

_____

_____

TRUE WORSHIP

"For I earnestly exhorted your fathers in the day I brought them up out of the land of Egypt, until this day, rising early and exhorting, saying, 'Obey My voice.'"
Jeremiah 11:7

"At my first reading it, I wondered what the author meant by saying 'That some falsely placed religion in going to church, doing hurt to no-one, being constantly in the duties of the (prayer) closet, and now and then reaching out their hands to give alms to their poor neighbors.' 'Alas!' thought I, ' if this be not true religion, what is?' God soon showed me; for in reading a few lines further, that 'true religion was union of the soul with God, and Christ formed within us,' a ray of divine light was instantaneously darted in upon my soul, and from that moment, but not till then, did I know that I must be a new creature." [7]

From George Whitefield's Journals

(He had been in the habit of praying and singing psalms five times each day, fasting every Friday, and receiving the sacrament of communion weekly at his church, yet he was not saved. He was a contemporary of John Wesley and went on to become one of the foremost evangelists of the 1700s.)

KEY STATEMENT: Are you a true worshiper?

Often in the Old Testament the Lord lamented that His people did not obey but followed the dictates of their own hearts. Consequently they would seek avenues to fulfill their own desires to the level of their own self-imagined boundaries that God would tolerate, thereby eliminating intimate fellowship with Him. It is possible for even the best among us to believe we're worshiping God when we're not.

Jeremiah 17:9 says, "The heart is deceitful above all things, and desperately wicked; who can know it?" When it comes to salvation and the things of God, don't make the mistake of trusting your own heart. Have God show you His heart. That's what you can journal today.

_____

_____

_____

_____

_____

_____

_____

_____

_____

Write this week's memory verse here: _____

_____

TRUE WORSHIP

Week 6 Day 38

"But the hour is coming, and now is, when the true worshipers will worship the Father in spirit and truth; for the Father is seeking such to worship Him.
God is Spirit, and those who worship Him must worship in spirit and truth."
John 4:23–24

"I went to America to convert the Indians; but O! who shall convert me?" [8]
John Wesley, January 24, 1738

KEY STATEMENT: Don't confuse a worship service with a life of worship.

It's rather humorous; we were delivered from the hymnals only to be bound to the large-screen projectors. So when you say the word *worship*, to most believers the first thing that comes to mind is slow songs on a CD, a music video, or in a service.

All week long God will speak to His children. He gives them direction to minister to their neighbor; asks them to give an offering or serve in their church or their community; or to minister to their family members and so forth. But they suppress His leading because they are too busy or want to enjoy what they are doing at the moment. Then they show up at church service and want something from God, namely blessings. They think they are worshiping God because they sing a few songs and tell God they love Him. This is not worship; it's just a slow song!

God is seeking true worshipers. Yesterday you saw how the great George Whitefield was very religious yet not saved. Another of the greatest ministers of the 1700s was Whitefield's friend, John Wesley. Wesley was an Oxford-educated ordained Anglican clergyman and a missionary, yet by his own admission he didn't know God! Only after he came to the knowledge of the truth was he soon converted and rocked the nation of England and the world.

Don't confuse a worship service with a life of obedience. Journal the ways God is drawing you now to a lifestyle of willing obedience.

TRUE WORSHIP

"Away with your hymns of praise! They are only noise to my ears. I will not listen to your music, no matter how lovely it is. Instead, I want to see a mighty flood of justice, a river of righteous living that will never run dry."
Amos 5:23–24, NLT

KEY STATEMENT: True worship is a life of obedience that renders the will of God to come forth on Earth.

It's so easy for us to get "the cart before the horse." We are used to doing things our own way. In America and western nations especially we are encouraged to be "our own man" or woman, to find our "own way." Even in the 1700s Whitefield was praying five times a day, fasting every Friday, and taking communion. Wesley was an educated minister. Yet both of them came to a saving knowledge of Christ *after* these things.

The same goes for today's church culture. Songs of worship, no matter how good or sincere, doesn't make for a life of obedience. Going to church, fasting, receiving communion doesn't necessarily equate to a life of worship. But out of a life of willing obedience will flow songs of worship that delight the heart of God rather than repulse Him as in the above scripture.

Have you ever seen this verse (Amos 5:23) in the scriptures before? _____

Does this verse surprise you when realize that God can be displeased with our

church services and worship music? _____

After you have meditated on these things, journal today how the Holy Spirit prompts you to change your lifestyle.

_____

_____

_____

_____

_____

_____

_____

_____

_____

_____

_____

TRUE WORSHIP

"Little children, let us not love [merely] in theory or in speech but in deed and in truth (in practice and in sincerity). By this we shall come to know (perceive, recognize, and understand) that we are of the Truth, and can reassure (quiet, conciliate, and pacify) our hearts in His presence."
I John 3:18–19, AMP

KEY STATEMENT: Willingness has to do with the attitude of our heart.

• One level of communication is our words. But a lifestyle of true worship will not only talk about serving God; there must be action as well.

"If I gave everything I have to the poor and even sacrificed my body, I could boast about it, but if I didn't love others, I would be of no value whatsoever."
I Corinthians 13:3, NLT

• Action is a higher level than mere words when it comes to communicating our faith, yet our outward actions can be deceiving. We can perform glorious deeds with no love in our heart.

"If you are willing and obedient, you shall eat the good of the land."
Isaiah 1:19

• The highest level of communication is that which proceeds from a willing and obedient heart. This is what Jesus refers to as truth.

John tells us in 1 John 3:19 we are to love God and mankind in action as well as truth, which is from the level of the heart.

How many times have we asked someone to do something only to have them appear submitted and obedient, yet all the while we know they're murmuring in their heart? And how many times have we done the same?

Let God search your heart. See if there are things you're doing outwardly while murmuring inwardly. The goal is to stand in His presence reassured in your heart that your love is not just in theory or speech, but is in deed and in truth.

_____

_____

_____

_____

_____

_____

_____

TRUE WORSHIP

Week 6 Day 41

"Trust in Him at all times, you people; pour out your heart before Him; God is a refuge for us."
Psalms 62:8

KEY STATEMENT: God draws near when we are gut-honest with Him.

This verse explains how God is seeking transparency in our relationship with Him. God wants us to come to Him and pour out our hearts to Him in open honesty so He can work in us to accomplish His will. This results in a life of true worship.

To worship God in truth is to not only to obey Him, but also to delight in what He has asked you to do.

What if George Whitefield and John Wesley had decided that because they were so religious or educated, they already knew God and didn't need the truth the Lord had brought to them? What if they had just kept on with their lives as usual? Besides ending up in hell themselves, millions of others would have never heard their messages that impacted the world. Instead, they were completely honest before the Lord and freely let go of their pride and worldly efforts, choosing instead to humble themselves before God.

How about you? What if you hadn't heeded the call of God? How many people would never have heard of Jesus because you didn't tell them? And how many people would never have benefited from the prayers you have offered on their behalf?

Your life makes a difference! People need your ministry and your prayers. Pour out your heart to God in total honesty. Praise, worship, and let Him know your deepest feelings. Be open to whatever He shows you, and let Him minister to you, journaling it here.

_____

_____

_____

_____

_____

_____

_____

_____

_____

_____

_____

_____

_____

TRUE WORSHIP

"The person who has my commandments and keeps them is the one who [really] loves Me, and whoever [really] loves me will be loved by My Father. And I [too] will love him and will show (reveal, manifest) Myself to him. [I will let Myself be clearly seen by him and make Myself real to him.]"
John 14:21, AMP

KEY STATEMENT: When you are obedient, God will make Himself known to you!

What an amazing scripture! It doesn't get any better than that. Those believers who worship God in spirit and truth—obey Him with willing and passionate hearts—are those who experience His abiding presence. These are the ones to whom God chooses to reveal Himself.

This odyssey you have embarked upon truly is an epic. It is your life story. And you don't have to live it on your own. God has promised—amazingly—to be with you every step of the way if you'll follow Him with passion and obedience.

FEET TO OUR FAITH: *Think about your journey thus far. Go over the scriptures you've chosen to memorize. Journal below what has taken place in your life and the lives of those around you. Put feet to your faith, and share today's amazing verse with someone you know. Also, tell someone who doesn't know the Lord about the story of Wesley and Whitefield—maybe God will use that story and your witness to save them, or at least you will plant a seed and another can water it. Either way, expect God to manifest Himself to you and on your behalf, and pray for those to whom He has you witness.*

_____

_____

_____

_____

_____

_____

_____

_____

_____

_____

_____

_____

TRUE WORSHIP

Additional Notes

WITH WHOM GOD DWELLS

"But He gives more grace. Therefore He says: 'God resists the proud, but gives grace to the humble.'... Humble yourselves in the sight of the Lord, and He will lift you up."
James 4:6, 10

KEY STATEMENT: God gives grace to those who humble themselves.

God earnestly desires our fellowship. One of His greatest desires is for a people to inhabit. James invites us to do more than just visit with God. He tells us God will lift us up to dwell in His presence continually. This is only available to the humble. Even more interesting is that God says it is we who humble ourselves.

We've been looking at verse 8 of James 4, *"Draw near to God and He will draw near to you."* Let's study a bit. Verse 8 is sandwiched between two verses about humility. Verse 8 shows that we have a part to play—we draw near first. Verse 10 also shows the same principle. We have a part to play—we humble ourselves in God's sight. Lastly, notice that God adds grace to grace—He gives more grace to those who have humbled themselves and received grace. **God keeps adding His blessings to those who obey Him. As you begin to obey God, you soon notice it becomes a habit that God Himself will reinforce with His grace!**

Meditate and worship today as you talk to the Lord about your part to play in each of these important truths. God put these all together for your admonition and your benefit, so let Him bless you with His Word!

Journal the insight God gives you today about these verses _____

_____

_____

_____

_____

_____

_____

_____

_____

_____

_____

_____

WITH WHOM GOD DWELLS

"The humble He guides in justice, and the humble He teaches His way."
Psalms 25:9

KEY STATEMENT: God will direct the path of the humble.

There are many in the body of Christ who do not understand the true meaning of humility. They think it means to be weak, wimpy, spineless, or even religious. Let's look at a biblical definition of humility.

Humility can be defined as "unconditional and instantaneous obedience to God." The people of Israel knew God's acts, but remember it was Moses who not only knew God's acts but the ways of God. Numbers 12:3 states, *"Moses was very humble, more than all men who were on the face of the earth."* Moses had chosen to leave a prestigious life behind in obedience to God. Time after time when confronting Pharaoh, and later in the wilderness, Moses was faced with tests and trials that demanded this kind of obedience to God.

Do you see how this fits with today's verse? It was Moses who was the most humble, and it was Moses who knew God's ways. If we would know His ways we must understand true humility. Biblical humility and obedience can't be separated.

Seek God today and ask Him to reveal to you the difference between the world's view of humility and the Bible's.

_____

_____

_____

_____

_____

_____

_____

_____

_____

_____

_____

_____

Write this week's memory verse here: _____

_____

WITH WHOM GOD DWELLS

Week 7, Day 45

"There is nothing in us that allows us to claim that we are capable of doing this work. The capacity we have comes from God."
2 Corinthians 3:5, TEV

"Now I am glad to boast about how weak I am; I am glad to be a living demonstration of Christ's power, instead of showing off my own power and abilities."
2 Corinthians 12:9, TLB

"As God is the ever-living, ever-present, ever-acting one—who upholds all things by the Word of His power, and in whom all things exist—the relationship of man to God could only be one of unceasing, absolute, universal dependence. As truly as God by His power once created, so truly by that same power must God, every moment, maintain. Man need only look back to the origin of human existence and he will acknowledge that he owes everything to God. Man's chief care, his highest virtue, and his only happiness, now and through all eternity, is to present himself as an empty vessel in which God can dwell and manifest His power and goodness." [9]
Andrew Murray

KEY STATEMENT: The second definition of humility is utter dependence on God.

Even Jesus said, *"The Son can do nothing of Himself"* (John 5:19). Christ became nothing that God might be all. He depended completely on the Father. He needed the Holy Spirit. If He, the immaculate Son of God, understood the necessity of humbling Himself in total surrender to God's provision, how much more must we!

Like everything, this comes back to matters of the heart. It is easy to talk about "trusting God." We may fool our friends and family (and perhaps even ourselves) that we are solely dependent on the Lord. But character is shown when things get tough. How easy it is to trust in a paycheck, until you get laid off. How simple it is to praise God, until trouble knocks. When your back is up against the proverbial wall is when your heart's condition is truly revealed. Don't wait to be humbled to learn of Him; humble yourself now with the knowledge of God.

Today let the Spirit of God search your heart. Ask God to reveal where you have need of true dependence on Him. An easy test is simply to imagine loss. Would your world fall apart, or would you draw closer to Jesus? Honesty here is crucial to your walk with God. Let God remove the veil of self-dependence in your ways. Let Him replace it with His peace—the peace that comes from knowing He Himself is all you truly need and that He is enough for you!

_____

_____

_____

_____

WITH WHOM GOD DWELLS

Week 7 Day 46

"For I am the least of the apostles, who am not worthy to be called an apostle."
1 Corinthians 15:9

"Yet not I, but the grace of God which was with me."
1 Corinthians 15:10

KEY STATEMENT: The humble understand it is God who works through them.

If anyone understood humility it was the apostle Paul. At one point he calls himself "least of the apostles," at another "least of all believers," and in 1 Timothy 1:15 he declares, "I am (not was) chief among sinners!" Paul constantly spoke of the fact that he was weak and lowly and that it was Christ working in him that accomplished any good works. He never lost sight of the great debt he owed Jesus, his Savior. Yet remember that Paul was perhaps the most accomplished apostle. Was he somehow speaking with false humility or political correctness? Hardly. He was speaking under the inspiration of the Holy Spirit because he was able to separate himself from his accomplishments. This brings us to our last definition of humility.

The third definition of humility is "the way you really see yourself." Paul viewed himself as we all should view ourselves—from God's perspective. Paul understood, as do all great saints, that all he had achieved flowed from God's ability through him.

What is your view of yourself? Have you really thought of this? Introspection is not something you hear much about in today's fast-paced, shallow, and materialistic culture, but a dose of it now and then is not only healthy, but it is also needed as long as it is done with the illumination of the Holy Spirit from God's Word.

Take some time today to dwell on these things as you worship God and write down how God would have you view yourself.

_____

_____

_____

_____

_____

_____

_____

_____

_____

_____

WITH WHOM GOD DWELLS

Week 7 Day 47

"Therefore, as the elect of God, holy and beloved, put on tender mercies,
kindness, humility, meekness, longsuffering."
Colossians 3:12

"Religion and virtue alike lend their sanctions to meekness and humility,
not only between men but between nations."
Winston Churchill

KEY STATEMENT: The most powerful of men and women are those who truly understand humility.

The fear of the Lord and humility are the power twins of the kingdom of God. History is filled with powerful men and women who understood the elevated position that humility holds in the lives of those who would do good.

The most powerful man that ever lived, the child of Joseph and Mary, the Son of God who was God Himself, was above all meek and lowly in heart. He spent time with little children to bless them. He made certain His mother Mary was cared for even as He hung from the cross in agony (John 19:26–27). He fed the poor and healed the sick, yet never had a place to lay His head or call His own. He could have called untold angels to His aid at any moment. When he stood before Pilate to be condemned, He told Pilate, "You have no power over Me except that which is given from heaven."

No man took the life of Jesus; He willingly offered it. It was in obedience to His Father that He gave Himself to be sacrificed. When you behold Him who has all power in heaven and earth, yet who humbled Himself at the death of the cross, you understand what true humility looks like. If you look at Jesus' life, it's remarkable. He was holy and beloved, full of tender mercies, kindness, humility, meekness, and longsuffering—and all the while being the most powerful man who ever lived.

These are the virtues we are to "put on." And we do this one way and one way only.

Draw near to God and He will draw near to you.

Journal today how Christ would have you be conformed to His image:

_____

_____

_____

_____

_____

_____

WITH WHOM GOD DWELLS

Week 7 Day 48

"But be ye doers of the word, and not hearers only, deceiving your own selves."
James 1:22, KJV

KEY STATEMENT: It is the humble with whom God dwells.

We've looked at three biblical definitions of humility:
- First and foremost it is our instant obedience to God.
- The second definition of humility is complete and utter dependence on God; we know we can't do anything apart from Him.
- The third definition of humility is the way you really see yourself.

 FEET TO OUR FAITH: These look good on paper, but let's put feet to your faith.

Think now, and pray. Then write out:
- Which, if any, of these three do you find easy?
- Which present you with continual difficulty? Why?

This journey is NOT about a mechanical process or a set of rules and formulas—it is about relationship with God Himself. Out of your dynamic relationship with God will flow rivers of living water. That's not hype—that's reality when you live a life of adventurous intimacy with the Holy Spirit.

In today's journal, write what the Lord shows you about your part in allowing Him to transform your life into one of humility—a life of instant obedience and complete dependence on Him.

_____

_____

_____

_____

_____

_____

_____

_____

_____

_____

It is the humble with whom God dwells!

WITH WHOM GOD DWELLS

*"This is the one I esteem: he who is humble and contrite in spirit,
and trembles at my word."*
Isaiah 66:2, NIV

"The hasty desire to rise is the cause of many a fall." [10]
Charles Spurgeon

(C.H. Spurgeon has been called the "prince of preachers," and his pulpit ministry during the 19th century
still impacts multitudes in the world today.)

KEY STATEMENT: God isn't looking for special people, he is looking for responsive people.

The Message by Eugene Peterson translates today's verse, *"There is something I'm looking for: a person simple and plain, reverently responsive to what I say."* God isn't looking for people who want to be great. The desire for position, popularity, power, fame, or riches has little to do with seeking God—and less to do with being found of Him.

Nor is God looking for those who pat themselves on the back because they're not seeking to be great. God won't be patronized. King David once prayed that he might be neither rich nor poor but rather content. King David, the man after God's own heart who would do all God's will, the great king and prophet, knew how to be found of God. Though he began as a humble shepherd boy and arose to the pinnacle of wealth and power, yet in the midst of it all he cried out to God. "I am broken and poor," he said. He wasn't speaking of wealth or power but rather the condition of his soul.

And there you have it—there is your secret. You can add it to the other treasures you have found on this journey. God Himself, the Ancient of Days, the Captain of the Host, the "I Am," chooses of His own volition to esteem some men and women more highly than the rest. Who? Read today's verse again and make it part of who you are.

Kneel before God in wonder and holy fear that you're privileged to read His Word and have Him dwell within you.

Journal your thoughts and other treasures from this seventh week of your journey to His heart:

_____

_____

_____

_____

_____

_____

WITH WHOM GOD DWELLS

Additional Notes

INTIMACY WITH THE HOLY SPIRIT

Week 8 Day 50

*"Or do you think that the Scripture says in vain,
'The Spirit who dwells in us yearns jealously'?"*
James 4:5

KEY STATEMENT: The Spirit, who is one person of the Godhead, dwells in you.

This scripture says the Spirit dwells in you and it is the Spirit who yearns jealously. Jesus is seated at the right hand of the Father in heaven. When Jesus ascended into heaven He sent the *Holy Spirit* to live, dwell, and make His abode in you. Isn't that wonderful news?

The definition for yearn is:
- To long intensely and persistently
- To feel tenderness or compassion
- To feel a tender or urgent longing

As the Holy Spirit longs and yearns for you, take time to do the same by recognizing the Holy Spirit's companionship at home, in the office, and in the countless other tasks that occupy your time.

Pray this prayer today:

Holy Spirit,

You are the focus in my life today.
I know that You live in me, and I recognize that You are a person of the Godhead. I yearn for Your friendship and companionship. Teach me and help me to understand the role that You have in my life. Thank You for making Your abode in me. You are my Helper whom the Father sent. Thank You for teaching me and bringing all things to my remembrance that You have said Amen.

Journal what the Holy Spirit shows you today:

_____

_____

_____

_____

_____

_____

_____

_____

_____

INTIMACY WITH THE HOLY SPIRIT

Week 8 Day 51

"Let Us make man in Our image, according to Our likeness."
Genesis 1:26

"You send forth Your Spirit, they are created."
Psalms 104:30

KEY STATEMENT: The Holy Spirit is a person, and we have been created in His image.

One of the reasons that we do not have intimacy with the Holy Spirit is because we have been taught a distorted image of the Holy Spirit. The Holy Spirit has been preached to be a "mystical" person of the Godhead.

One of the first impressions most people have of the Holy Spirit is a dove. The Holy Spirit is described as a dove in the Gospels, but just because He descended upon Jesus "like a dove" does not make the Holy Spirit an actual dove.

The Holy Spirit is a person of the Godhead. Read these scriptures about the Holy Spirit and meditate on them. The Holy Spirit:
- Has a mind (Rom. 8:27)
- Has a will (1 Cor. 12:11)
- Has emotions (Rom. 15:30)
- Speaks (Heb. 3:7; 1 Tim. 4:1)
- Teaches (1 Cor. 2:13)
- Can be grieved (Eph. 4:30)
- Can be insulted (Heb. 10:29)
- Can be lied to just like any human (Acts 5)

The Holy Spirit is wonderful, and we have been created in His image.

Pray this prayer today:

Holy Spirit,

I am sorry if I have taken You for granted. Help me to recognize You working in my life and speaking to me on my journey. May the grace of the Lord Jesus Christ, the love of God, and the communion of the Holy Spirit be with me today. Amen.

*Write this week's memory verse here*_____

_____

_____

_____

_____

INTIMACY WITH THE HOLY SPIRIT

Week 8, Day 52

"Who has directed the Spirit of the LORD, or as His counselor has informed him? With whom did He consult and who gave Him understanding? And who taught Him in the path of justice and taught Him knowledge, and informed Him of the way of understanding?"
Isaiah 40:13–14, NAS

KEY STATEMENT: God's wisdom, knowledge, and understanding are limitless, and He yearns to teach you what He knows.

Intimacy with the Holy Spirit is developed by communication, which is the avenue to a strong friendship. Those in your life you are the closest to are the ones that you have communicated with for endless amounts of time. They are the ones who know you best, and they are the ones whom you know best.

The Spirit of God desires to be your closest friend. He yearns for your fellowship. He desires to teach you what He knows, and His knowledge is infinite!

When you know something of great value, you passionately desire to share it with those you are close with and love. The Holy Spirit is no different. The Holy Spirit wants to share with you what He knows!

Pray this prayer:

Holy Spirit,

Lead and direct me in the things of God, for I know You are one with Jesus and the Father. Be my counselor who informs me of my life direction. Give me understanding that I may know which way I am to go. Direct my paths and make them straight. Teach me justice and righteousness. Be my closest friend. Amen.

Journal what the Holy Spirit shows you today:

_____

_____

_____

_____

_____

_____

_____

_____

Week 8 Day 53

"Oh, there is so much more I want to tell you, but you can't bear it now. When the Spirit of truth comes, he will guide you into all truth. He will not be presenting his own ideas; he will be telling you what he has heard. He will tell you about the future. He will bring me glory by revealing to you whatever he receives from me. All that the Father has is mine; this is what I mean when I say that the Spirit will reveal to you whatever he receives from me."
John 16:12-15, NLT

KEY STATEMENT: The Holy Spirit guides you into all truth.

The glorious thing about the Holy Spirit residing on the inside of you is that He does not have to sleep, eat, or take breaks. You can speak to the Holy Spirit any time of the day or night, wherever you are, and you don't have to wait for others to finish before it is your turn. You have His complete and undivided attention at all times! The Holy Spirit has the ability to communicate personally with anyone who is hungry and calls upon Him.

Even though the Father, Son, and Holy Spirit are three distinct persons, each with their own mind, will, and emotions, they are still completely one. You will never find them differing, and you will always find them one in purpose, plan, and execution of will.

Pray this prayer:

Father, Son, and Holy Spirit,

I worship You. I am glad that I have the three of You in my life and that You said in Your Word that You would never leave or forsake me. I need the truth of the Word and the Spirit in my life today and every day. Guide me into all truth. Thank You for telling me the truth and all things I need to know from the Father. I thank You for revealing Yourself to me so that I may walk in purity of heart. Help me to know You more. Amen.

Journal what the Holy Spirit shows you today:

_____

_____

_____

_____

_____

_____

_____

_____

INTIMACY WITH THE HOLY SPIRIT

Week 8 Day 54

"The grace of the Lord Jesus Christ, and the love of God, and the communion of the Holy Spirit be with you all. Amen."
2 Corinthians 13:14

KEY STATEMENT: The Holy Spirit is your constant companion.

Grace is attributed to the role of Jesus in our lives. Love is attributed to the role of God in our lives. *Communion* is attributed to the role of the Holy Spirit in our lives.

Webster's dictionary describes fellowship as "companionship, company, the quality or state of being comradely." Here are some ways that communion can be described in your relationship with the Holy Spirit:
- Fellowship
- Sharing together
- Partnership or joint participation
- Close mutual association
- Intimacy

Take time today to study the scriptures listed below. Study the role and the work of the Holy Spirit in the lives of the apostles. The New Testament servants of God were very aware of the Spirit of God's constant companionship with them. God desires to reveal and share deep and intimate things to you through His Spirit.

- Paul (Acts 16:6–7; 20:22–23)
- Philip (Acts 8:29)
- Peter (Acts 10:19–20)

Pray this prayer:

Holy Spirit,

I know that Your grace, love, and communion are available to me whenever I need them. You have given me the ability always to do the right thing. I will continue to fight the good fight of faith. Thank You for hearing me and filling me with Your supernatural power so that I may be able to accomplish Your plan for me on this journey to Your heart. Amen.

Journal what the Holy Spirit shows you today:

_____

_____

_____

_____

_____

INTIMACY WITH THE HOLY SPIRIT

Week 8 Day 55

"But I make known to you, brethren, that the gospel which was preached by me is not according to man. For I neither received it from man, nor was I taught it, but it came through the revelation of Jesus Christ."
Galatians 1:11–12

"Our first work, therefore, ought to be to come into God's presence not with our ignorant prayers, not with many words and thoughts, but in the confidence that the divine work of the Holy Spirit is being carried on within us. This confidence will encourage reverence and quietness and will also enable us, in dependence on the help which the Spirit gives, to lay our desires and heart-needs before God. The great lesson for every prayer is—see to it, first of all, that you commit yourself to the leading of the Holy Spirit, and with entire dependence on Him, give Him the first place. For through Him your prayer will have a value you cannot imagine, and through Him also you will learn to speak out your desires in the name of Christ." [11]
Andrew Murray, April 1912
(Because of his intimate walk with God and prolific writings, Dutch Reformed Pastor Andrew Murray is considered a father of faith to countless persons worldwide.) [11]

KEY STATEMENT: The Holy Spirit in you will reveal Jesus to you.

The apostle Paul never walked side by side with Jesus as did Peter and the others. And Paul didn't receive his knowledge from the other apostles either. Paul says he *"conferred not with flesh and blood"* (Gal. 1:16). He came to know Jesus by the revelation of the Holy Spirit. Paul's intimacy with Jesus was such that even Peter said that some of Paul's writings were hard to be understood (2 Pet. 3:15–16)!

Like in Paul's day, Jesus is not with us in flesh and blood. It is actually better that way, Jesus told us, because He sent the Holy Spirit to be with us and in us (John 16:7). You can know Jesus by the revelation of the Holy Spirit as He reveals God's Word to you.

Here is today's prayer:

Father, in Jesus' name I come to You today. I worship You in the power of the Holy Spirit. Lord, show me the scriptures I need to be more like Jesus. Reveal Yourself to me as You did for Paul, so I may have intimacy with You and be conformed to Your image. Spirit of God, I commit to do my part to be faithful in prayer and communion with You every day. I need You and depend on You to assist and empower me with the discipline and passion I need to press in to You daily. Amen.

INTIMACY WITH THE HOLY SPIRIT

*"My heart has heard you say, 'Come talk with me.' And my
heart responds, 'LORD, I am coming.'"*
Psalms 27:8, NLT

*"On the first of May in the olden times, according to annual custom, many inhabitants of London
went into the fields to bathe their faces with the early dew upon the grass under the idea that it
would render them beautiful. Some writers call the custom superstitious. It may have been so, but
this we know, that to bathe one's face every morning in the dew of heaven by prayer and
communion, is the sure way to obtain true beauty of life and character."* [12]
Charles Spurgeon

KEY STATEMENT: : The Holy Spirit is calling you and awaiting your response.

Spurgeon, "the prince of preachers," said it beautifully: "This we know, that to bathe one's
face every morning in the dew of heaven by prayer and communion, is the sure way to
obtain true beauty of life and character." This quest you are on is exactly about that: living
the beauty and character of a *lifestyle* of intimacy with God.

You are in this race to finish well, not to live a life of hit-or-miss or inconsistency.
It's all about co-mingling with the very Spirit of God. You and He are
one in Christ. Your life can be bathed in His presence, His peace, His
calm, His power, His knowledge, His strength, His gifts…and more! He
is God! Take your fill of Him today and each day!

In today's prayer, let your enthusiasm burst forth! *Dig deep* if you have to and call it forth,
stirring yourself up in your most holy faith.

*Father God, in Jesus' name I come today accepting Your invitation to be filled with You, Your Spirit. You
are Almighty God! You want me to do this. I am drawing near, and I trust You to draw near to me. Help
me to develop the habit of digging deep when I need to. Help me to honor You and know You and hear from
You every day. I am cultivating a life of intimacy with You, Lord, and I am blessed and excited and ready
to move forward!*

Keep praying and then journal what the Lord shows you this last day of the week.

_____

_____

_____

_____

_____

_____

_____

INTIMACY WITH THE HOLY SPIRIT

Additional Notes

THE PROMISE OF THE FATHER

"He said unto them, Have ye received the Holy Ghost since ye believed? And they said unto him, We have not so much as heard whether there be any Holy Ghost."
Acts 19:2, KJV

Just as my soul has my whole body for its dwelling-place and service, so the Holy Spirit would have my body and soul as His dwelling place, entirely under His control. No one can continue long and earnestly in prayer without beginning to perceive that the Spirit is gently leading to an entirely new consecration, of which previously he knew nothing. [13]
Andrew Murray, April 1912

KEY STATEMENT: Being saved is one thing; being filled with the Holy Spirit is another.

Countless multitudes in the church make the mistake of believing experience rather than truth. Experience may confirm truth, but it is not to be a teacher of truth. The Holy Spirit leads and guides us into truth, and He always agrees with the written Word of God. Don't get it backwards, wanting to experience and then believe.

The simple truth is that many believers have been saved by Christ but haven't heard or have heard incorrectly about the Holy Ghost. In this coming week's devotions you will again see the reality of a journey to His heart. You'll study a subject so desperately needed in the church during the time of the Book of Acts and even more so today—the infilling of the Holy Spirit.

Believing in the Word of God concerning being filled with the Holy Spirit will bring you to a new and fresh level of intimacy with God. Be open and teachable as you continue this journey in God's Word.

Pray this prayer:

Father God, I come to You in the name of Jesus. I pray this week You will give me understanding and enlightenment as I open my heart to learn of You. Help me to know an entirely new consecration. Holy Spirit, lead me and guide me into all truth. I know this is why You were sent to me. Lord, I don't want to experience then believe. I will believe the Word of God, then see and experience. Amen.

_____

_____

_____

_____

DVD Extra Feature

The next step on your journey to intimacy with the Holy Spirit is the infilling of the Holy Spirit in your life. Turn to page 241 and read Appendix B ("How to Be Filled With the Holy Spirit") in your Drawing Near book.
Enter code: **767**, *to watch this bonus feature in Lesson 9 of your DVD.*

THE PROMISE OF THE FATHER

Week 9 Day 58

"But you shall receive power when the Holy Spirit has come upon you; and you shall be witnesses to Me in Jerusalem, and in all Judea and Samaria, and to the end of the earth."
Acts 1:8

KEY STATEMENT: Being filled with the Holy Spirit will give you the impact of the Holy Spirit.

All throughout the Book of Acts you see it again and again; people were saved, then filled with the Holy Spirit, and everywhere they went they made a noticeable impact for God. The fact that they were filled with the Holy Spirit was not only evident because they had the fruit of the Holy Spirit (love, joy, peace, etc.) and the gifts of the Holy Spirit such as tongues, prophecy, and miracles, but you could also say they had the *impact of a Spirit-filled life.*

It is common among believers when they are first saved that they are "on fire" for a while. They tell their friends about Jesus, and people are added to the kingdom. But then the initial fervor wears off, and often years go by with no outward fruit of witnessing to anyone. But that is not what you see in the Book of Acts.

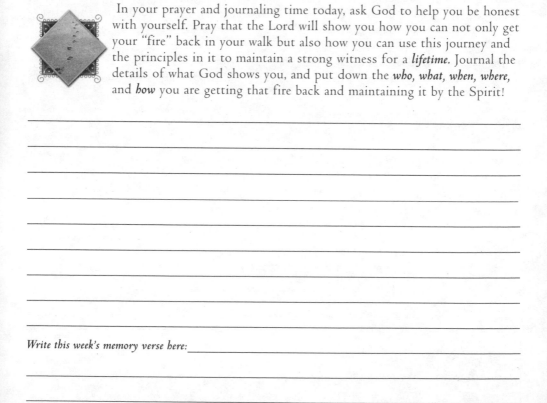 In your prayer and journaling time today, ask God to help you be honest with yourself. Pray that the Lord will show you how you can not only get your "fire" back in your walk but also how you can use this journey and the principles in it to maintain a strong witness for a *lifetime.* Journal the details of what God shows you, and put down the *who, what, when, where,* and *how* you are getting that fire back and maintaining it by the Spirit!

_____

_____

_____

_____

_____

_____

_____

_____

_____

*Write this week's memory verse here:*_____

_____

_____

THE PROMISE OF THE FATHER

Week 9, Day 59

"Likewise the Spirit also helps in our weaknesses. For we do not know what we should pray for as we ought, but the Spirit Himself makes intercession for us with groanings which cannot be uttered."
Romans 8:26

"In what degree are we to expect the Spirit of God to affect the minds of believers? The text says: 'The Spirit maketh intercession with groanings that cannot be uttered.' The meaning of this I understand to be, that the Spirit excites, desires too great to be uttered except by groans—making the soul too full to utter its feelings by words, so that the person can only groan them out to God, who understands the language of the heart."

"Many Christians are so ignorant of the Spirit's influences, and have thought so little about having His assistance in prayer, that when they have such influences they do not know it, and so do not yield to them, and cherish them." [14]
Charles Finney speaking of Romans 8:26, from Revivals of Religion

KEY STATEMENT: If you are going to be filled and used by the Holy Spirit, you must first believe and yield to Him.

Something caused you to take this Drawing Near journey. "Someone" is actually the better way to put it, and of course, it was the Holy Spirit. You yielded to Him, giving Him first place in your life and setting aside the necessary time.

If you're still not sure about the infilling of the Holy Spirit, read chapter 11 again from the book and watch session 9 on the DVD, and/or speak with someone you know who is filled with the Spirit with the evidence of speaking in tongues.

There is no reason for us today to be ignorant of the Spirit's influences. Recognize that He is leading you and influencing you right now to yield your heart, mind, and lips to Him in prayer.

Experience is a result of God's Word. You've read the book, studied your Bible, and watched the DVD. Now it's time to journal your experience as you spend time in prayer today:

_____

_____

_____

_____

_____

_____

THE PROMISE OF THE FATHER

Week 9 Day 60

"How God anointed Jesus of Nazareth with the Holy Spirit and with power, who went about doing good and healing all who were oppressed by the devil, for God was with Him."
Acts 10:38

"Then Jesus arrived from Nazareth, anointed by God with the Holy Spirit, ready for action. He went through the country helping people and healing everyone who was beaten down by the Devil. He was able to do all this because God was with Him."
Acts 10:38, The Message

KEY STATEMENT: When you are filled with the Holy Spirit, you'll live a Jesus lifestyle.

Do you want to walk in the anointing and power of Jesus? It is by the power of the Holy Spirit that you will. The Spirit gives you power to be a witness. The Spirit gives you power to go "through the country helping people and healing all those who are beaten down by the Devil."

The question is:
- Do you believe it?
- Are you a man or woman "ready for action"?
- Will you yield to Him?
- What is the level of your desire?

Press on. Go further, faster, and stronger than you ever have. Don't spend another minute of your life waiting to draw near, waiting to be anointed. Go into your prayer closet now, boldly call out to God, thanking Him for sending the promise of the Holy Spirit to you. Worship Him as God Almighty, bow before Him in the fear of the Lord, humble yourself in His presence as you seek Him. Then allow Him to come and fill you with Himself. Now go; be like Jesus. Go about doing good and living a lifestyle of the power of the Spirit!

_____

_____

_____

_____

_____

_____

_____

_____

_____

_____

_____

_____

THE PROMISE OF THE FATHER

Week 9 Day 61

"Then Peter said to them, 'Repent, and let every one of you be baptized in the name of Jesus Christ for the remission of sins; and you shall receive the gift of the Holy Spirit. For the promise is to you and to your children, and to all who are afar off, as many as the Lord our God will call.'"
Acts 2:38–39

KEY STATEMENT: The promise of the Holy Spirit is for all believers.

This devotional, the Drawing Near book itself, and the many teachings on the videos are truly a wealth of information. Praise the Lord that you have been given this treasure. Perhaps the greatest blessing of being filled with the Holy Spirit is the supernatural ability that comes with Him to reach out and help others.

FEET TO OUR FAITH: *We've talked about people who know the Lord but haven't received the Holy Spirit.*

Today write down:
- The name of someone you know who needs to be filled with the Holy Spirit with the evidence of speaking in tongues. _____
- Now ask the Lord to make you bold and give you the words and opportunity to share with them what you've learned on this journey so they can receive the baptism of the Holy Spirit.
- Make sure you seek God to get the details necessary—details only God could know—of just how to minister to this person.

Journal the details God gives you, and make sure you are faithful to follow through on it. Truly you are anointed and ready for action!

_____

_____

_____

_____

_____

_____

_____

_____

_____

THE PROMISE OF THE FATHER

Week 9 Day 62

"But you, beloved, building yourselves up on your most holy faith,
praying in the Holy Spirit."
Jude 20

"If you praise him in the private language of tongues, God understands you but no one else does, for you are sharing intimacies just between you and him."
1 Corinthians 14:2, The Message

KEY STATEMENT: Tongues for personal prayer is the Father's provision for every Christian who believes.

In his book and videos, John teaches in-depth about the Holy Spirit and tongues. There are four different categories of tongues. Two are for public ministry, and two are for personal fellowship with God. Since this is devotional time, we will look at one of the two categories for personal fellowship.

Praying in your known language is great; it's awesome to fellowship with God. Now think of fellowshiping with Him in your own private language of tongues, just you and God, intimate, passionate, in secret. Building yourself up on your most holy faith—the more you pray the stronger you build—it doesn't get any better than that!

Meditate on that, and journal what the Lord shows you today as you praise Him in the private language of tongues.

_____

_____

_____

_____

_____

_____

_____

_____

_____

_____

_____

_____

_____

THE PROMISE OF THE FATHER

Week 9 Day 63

"And the Holy Spirit helps us in our distress. For we don't even know what we should pray for, nor how we should pray. But the Holy Spirit prays for us with groanings that cannot be expressed in words."
Romans 8:26, NLT

KEY STATEMENT: God has provided our prayer language to pray for things we don't understand or have knowledge of.

Yesterday you looked at one of the two categories for personal fellowship with God. The second is tongues for intercession. This is when you pray for others. On day 59 we quoted Finney as he talked about yielding to the Spirit's influences. Simply put, God is all-knowing, and we are not. Through your heavenly prayer language, God will use you—if you yield to Him—to pray on behalf of others.

The way you learn to yield to the Holy Spirit is the same as any relationship. You spend quality time together. As you build your relationship, you will become more sensitive and responsive to the leading of the Holy Spirit, and you will receive the great blessing of being His vessel to pray for others. Expect great miracles as you give yourself to this kind of prayer. God knows whose life could be saved or changed as you yield to the Holy Spirit!

Ask the Spirit today to give you an opportunity to bring God glory. Journal all you see in the Spirit.

_____

_____

_____

_____

_____

_____

_____

_____

_____

_____

_____

_____

_____

_____

_____

THE LANGUAGE OF INTIMACY

Additional Notes

_____
_____
_____
_____
_____
_____
_____
_____
_____
_____
_____
_____
_____
_____
_____
_____
_____
_____
_____
_____
_____
_____
_____
_____
_____
_____
_____
_____
_____

THE LANGUAGE OF INTIMACY

Week 10 Day 64

"If you then, being evil, know how to give good gifts to your children, how much more will your heavenly Father give the Holy Spirit to those who ask Him!"
Luke 11:13

"I wish you all spoke with tongues."
1 Corinthians 14:5

"But if anyone is ignorant, let him be ignorant. Therefore, brethren, desire earnestly to prophesy, and do not forbid to speak with tongues."
1 Corinthians 14:38–39

KEY STATEMENT: The main purpose of tongues is intimacy.

God wants our interaction with Him to be lush and rich. God has given us a way to communicate intimately and fellowship with Him on a deep level, a level that our natural unredeemed minds could never reach.

In 1 Corinthians 14:2 Paul said, *"He who speaks in a tongue does not speak to men but to God."* The Message translates this, *"If you praise him in the private language of tongues, God understands you but no one else does, for you are sharing intimacies just between you and him."* That is as plain as you could ask for and as wondrous as the gospel itself.

Take some time today to just pray, worship, and journal. What have you been going through, and how can God help? Draw near to Him, and He will draw near to you.

_____

_____

_____

_____

_____

_____

_____

_____

_____

_____

_____

_____

_____

_____

THE LANGUAGE OF INTIMACY

"I thank my God I speak with tongues more than you all."
1 Corinthians 14:18

KEY STATEMENT: Paul prayed in tongues a great deal, and so should you.

Check this out! Here is how *The Message* **translation puts the above verse.**
"I'm grateful to God for the gift of praying in tongues that he gives us for praising him, which leads to wonderful intimacies we enjoy with him. I enter into this as much or more than any of you."

Hallelujah! Jump and shout and praise the Lord! Look at the apostle Paul's life. When he was saved and filled with the Holy Spirit, he changed from a murderous, hyper-religious fanatic to a humble, self-controlled, and mighty servant of Jesus. Paul said it was the revelation of Jesus Christ by the Spirit that made him what he was. Paul was a man who prayed with tongues as much or more than any in the whole church he wrote to!

Just think what God can do in and for, by and through you, too. God is no respecter of persons. No, you may not be a world missionary (or maybe you are!), you may not have a title or lofty position, and maybe none but a few know your name. But that's the beauty of it.

Yesterday we noted that when you speak in tongues you are speaking directly to God. He's not interested in titles or positions. He's interested in YOU! He is always ready for you to simply open your mouth and pray. Do that now and journal.

_____

_____

_____

_____

_____

_____

_____

_____

_____

_____

_____

Write this week's memory verse here: _____

_____

_____

THE LANGUAGE OF INTIMACY

 *Week 10, Day 66*

"For he who speaks in a tongue does not speak to men but to God, for no one understands him; however, in the spirit he speaks mysteries."
I Corinthians 14:2

KEY STATEMENT: God reveals mysteries through praying in tongues.

Are you having trouble in your life? Are things going on you don't understand? Does God's Word seem dry? Has life got you down?

The Greek word for mysteries here is musterion. According to W. E. Vines Expository Dictionary of *New Testament Words,* "in the ordinary sense a mystery implies knowledge withheld; its scriptural significance is truth revealed."

One of the many benefits of praying in tongues is that God already knows what we need. What is a mystery to us sure isn't to Him. He also knows what everyone else needs, so we see again how tongues can benefit those for whom we intercede in prayer. Another benefit is the Holy Spirit will reveal truths from God's Word to us. As we pray in tongues, illumination concerning the mysteries of God's Word comes and sheds light where our understanding was previously dim.

Thanks be to God for this amazing gift! Take advantage of it now and daily. Ask God to reveal Himself to you now, and journal what He tells you.

_____

_____

_____

_____

_____

_____

_____

_____

_____

_____

_____

_____

_____

_____

THE LANGUAGE OF INTIMACY

"Counsel in the heart of man is like deep water, but a man of understanding will draw it out."
Proverbs 20:5

KEY STATEMENT: You choose whether or not you are a man or woman of understanding.

If you have ever lived on a farm with a well, you know that sometimes the water just seemed to stop. It's not because there was no water there or the well ran dry. It's because the pump "lost its prime." Once you "get the prime back" and start pumping again, suddenly it's a gusher and the water flows freely.

When no one knows the problem is with the prime, everyone stands around looking at each other saying, "Bless God, I guess we are out of water. The well's dry, and there's nothing there." But when Dad comes around, he immediately understands the problem and draws the water out once again. Dad understands too that you don't stop once there is a little trickle. You keep the prime going until you are at full flow.

So it is with God. He's never dry. He's never out of living water. Don't be like those with no understanding, standing around insulting the character of the well. Be a man or woman of understanding and draw out the life and wisdom of God by priming the pump in the Spirit through prayer. Don't settle for a trickle. Keep the prime going until you are at full flow.

Pray this prayer:

Lord, in Jesus' name, I ask for a divine river to flow freely out of me. Help me to "prime the pump" in my life. I want to be filled to overflowing so that I may know You intimately. Help me to understand Your heart and Your counsel. Teach me to be obedient so that I may continually draw counsel out so that I may be filled with life and wisdom. Let me be a light to others and use the gifts You have placed on the inside of me.

_____

_____

_____

_____

_____

_____

_____

THE LANGUAGE OF INTIMACY

*"For with stammering lips and another tongue He will speak to this people,
to whom He said, 'This is the rest with which you may cause the weary to rest,' and,
'This is the refreshing'; yet they would not hear."*
Isaiah 28:11 12

KEY STATEMENT: God has a rest for those who hear Him.

Let's be real. Life can be hard. Circumstances can seem to conspire against the best of us. You're tough, but the world tells you it's tougher. But wait a minute; you're not of this world. You're translated out of the kingdom of darkness into the kingdom of His dear Son. You know God. In fact, to the envy of the world, you have a direct line every moment of every day to the King of the universe.

Here is the refreshing. If you are weary, get some rest. How? By sleeping? By taking the day off? No. The rest we are speaking of provides more than a temporary respite from the world. Open your ears, and hear the word of the Lord. He's ready to speak to you now and give you a spiritual refreshing, power from on high that transcends the things of the earth.

Enter into rest. Jesus gives it to you now. Relax and pour out your heart to God. It's going to be OK, because He's in charge of your destiny. Today's prayer is the calm in the eye of the storm. Pray in the Spirit and yield to His peace.

THE LANGUAGE OF INTIMACY

"But solid food belongs to those who are of full age, that is, those who by reason of use have their senses exercised to discern both good and evil."
Hebrews 5:14

KEY STATEMENT: Those who develop a habit of much prayer have the sharpest spiritual senses.

Just as we have five natural senses, we have five spiritual senses—taste, touch, smell, sight, and hearing. We often read of these in the Scriptures. What does it mean to taste and see that the Lord is good? If you have walked with the Lord for a while or you have learned the power of prayer, chances are you are not in the dark as to what Scripture means when it speaks of spiritual senses. You've "tasted of the goodness of the Lord," you've "seen the light," you've "drunk the living water," and you've "heard the sound of the mighty rushing wind."

If these terms are new to you, it's not that difficult. Just as an athlete, musician, gemstone specialist, or wine taster has learned the nuances of their respective calling, so you can exercise and develop your spiritual senses. You do this through the Word of God, obedience to the Word, and prayer. *Specifically, much prayer in the Spirit, in other tongues, will develop your spiritual senses.*

Today either spend some serious time praying in other tongues or schedule an early morning or other time to do that. Let God speak to you through the Scriptures and the Spirit about this as you do.

_____

_____

_____

_____

_____

_____

_____

_____

_____

_____

_____

_____

_____

_____

THE LANGUAGE OF INTIMACY

Week 10 Day 70

"And He said to them, 'Go into all the world and preach the gospel to every creature. He who believes and is baptized will be saved; but he who does not believe will be condemned. And these signs will follow those who believe: In My name they will cast out demons; they will speak with new tongues.'"
Mark 16:15–17

KEY STATEMENT: Praying in tongues empowers you.

Don't draw back from the gift of the Holy Spirit. No matter your age or background, or how long you've been saved, you can build your inner man through praying in tongues and asking for the interpretation (1 Cor. 14:13) as you pray that your understanding may receive the benefit of communion with the Holy Spirit.

Worship God and pray; sing and raise your hands. The cares of the world will gradually fall away, and the counsel of God will replace them. Then boldly record in your journal what God reveals. You'll see the mysteries of God unfold in your life and the lives of those around you. Even the lives of people you may never meet can be touched as you pray in the Holy Ghost! Go now into the entire world. First in prayer, then out into your mission field—where you work, where you play—wherever God has called you!

Trust now—you have what it takes—you have the Holy Spirit!!

_____

_____

_____

_____

_____

_____

_____

_____

_____

_____

_____

_____

_____

_____

THE LANGUAGE OF INTIMACY

Additional Notes

FULL ASSURANCE OF FAITH

"Let us draw near with a true heart in full assurance of faith, having our hearts sprinkled from an evil conscience and our bodies washed with pure water."
Hebrews 10:22

KEY STATEMENT: To hear from God and experience His presence you must come to Him in full assurance of faith.

Jesus. 100 percent man, 100 percent God. No one took His life from Him; He offered it up freely. His royal blood was shed, He hung on the cross, and now He's seated at the right hand of God. The deal is done. God dealt the devil a losing hand, and if you're born again, you're no longer a child of darkness but a genuine child of God Himself.

Your relationship with God doesn't have to be an up-and-down, hit-or-miss scenario. By now you've probably memorized James 4:8: *"Draw near to God and He will draw near to you."* It's a *promise for every believer.*

Faced with the news that his daughter was already declared dead, the ruler of the synagogue didn't get what you might expect from Jesus. No sermon, no rebuke, and no *"I'm sorry."* Jesus simply said, *"Do not be afraid; only believe"* (Mark 5:36). Bystanders may have ridiculed Jesus, but the father believed, and his daughter received new life. And so God is saying to you right now, "Be not afraid; only believe. Enter into My presence in full assurance of faith. I will personally meet you there and fill you with new life."

For today's prayer time, ask the Holy Spirit to reveal to you anything that is keeping you back from approaching the throne of God boldly and without fear or doubt. Get your business straight with God and journal it. He's waiting. Only believe.

_____

_____

_____

_____

_____

_____

_____

_____

_____

_____

_____

FULL ASSURANCE OF FAITH

Week 11 Day 72

"It's impossible to please God apart from faith. And why? Because anyone who wants to approach God must believe both that he exists and that he cares enough to respond to those who seek him."
Hebrews 11:6, The Message

KEY STATEMENT: If you call upon Him in faith, God will respond to you today.

We know that God exists, but sometimes we wonder if He is listening or if He really cares for us. With everyday routines and cares, we sometimes forget to take the time to respond to Him in prayer. We lose the passion of our faith and thus our ability to believe and not doubt. That is why it is so important to take the time continually to come into His presence, praying in the spirit and building yourself up on your most holy faith.

The Word tells us that it is "impossible to please God apart from faith." God does care for you, and He does desire to respond to those who seek Him. But He responds to faith, not need. **Here's a short list of the types of things that create barriers between God and us:**
- Hidden sin
- Addictions that seem impossible to overcome
- Complacency
- Lack of time
- Lack of knowledge

Whatever your story, it's first between you and God. Jesus came to give abundant life. He didn't come to call "the righteous" but sinners. It's funny. That's actually really good news because we all qualify as sinners. Take your story to God. He does care. Furthermore, He proved He cares by sending His very own Son. Don't let that sacrifice go to waste.

Today enter in by the blood of Jesus. He cares enough to respond to YOU.

_____

_____

_____

_____

_____

_____

Write this week's memory verse here: _____

_____

_____

FULL ASSURANCE OF FAITH

"As it is written, 'The just shall live by faith.'"
Romans 1:17

KEY STATEMENT: Living by faith is a *lifestyle*.

Martin Luther's revelation of this short verse literally changed civilization as we know it. On April 16, 1521 he was on his way to stand before a council to receive what he believed would be a death sentence. He had good reason to believe that, as others had been martyred before him. As he entered the city, crowds thronged, and General Frundsburg, the outstanding soldier of Germany, said, "My poor monk! My little monk! Thou art on thy way to make a stand such as I and many of my knights have never done in our toughest battles." When Luther was asked if he would recant what he had written in his books, he replied, "I will never deny any of them." As he finished his second day of inquiry, he was again asked if he would revoke or not. As he risked cruel and torturous death, here are the last words of his now immortal reply:

"...my conscience has been taken captive by these words of God. I cannot revoke anything, nor do I wish to; since to go against one's conscience is neither safe nor right; here I stand, I cannot do otherwise. God help me. Amen." [15]

God did help him. Amazingly he was spared, and the world forever changed.

Facing death, Luther entered boldly with full assurance of faith and stood before rulers of men.
God has given us a "great cloud of witnesses" as examples of the faith. It is not a sentence of death but the gift of life we face. We stand accused before no council of men, but forgiven we come before the King of kings. It is not demanded we recant; we are exhorted to believe. Let us throw ourselves down and worship this Great King who came among us as one of us and calls us to Himself!

Worship Him and journal as you go to Him in faith.

_____

_____

_____

_____

_____

_____

_____

_____

_____

_____

FULL ASSURANCE OF FAITH

"Therefore, brethren, having boldness to enter the Holiest by the blood of Jesus, by a new and living way which He consecrated for us, through the veil, that is, His flesh, and having a High Priest over the house of God, let us draw near with a true heart in full assurance of faith, having our hearts sprinkled from an evil conscience and our bodies washed with pure water. Let us hold fast the confession of our hope without wavering, for He who promised is faithful."

Hebrews 10:19–23

KEY STATEMENT: Hope is not a "maybe so" word. It is "a confident expectation."

Martin Luther's story is so powerful. You might not be reading this right now if it wasn't for the Reformation! When he read, "The just shall live by faith," he didn't see it as just ink on a page or a Sunday sermon. He was a Catholic monk, and this "new" truth profoundly changed everything about his life. For Luther, living by faith was the center of his universe as he faced the political and religious forces of his world.

Luther discovered what we all must. God hasn't called us to some religion made up by men or some faith that worships a dead god. God hasn't given us a set of rules or religious duties by which we will be saved. Luther "got it." The provision God gave for salvation was Himself. And faith alone in that gift brings us to righteousness.

We've said it again and again—this journey is not about a formula—it's about relationship. Let a little of Luther's valor rub off on you today. Let the same true heart that was in Jesus, the apostles, and Luther be found in you as you draw near to God in full assurance of faith. Don't "hope so"; know so.

FULL ASSURANCE OF FAITH

Week 11 Day 75

"So then faith comes by hearing, and hearing by the word of God."
Romans 10:17

KEY STATEMENT: You increase your faith by hearing God's Word.

This is not complicated. In the Gospels when the apostles asked Jesus to increase their faith, He likened it to a seed. We've all seen a tiny seed planted in dry ground and left to itself. What happens? Nothing. Take that same seed and care for it properly, and you can grow a mighty oak.

The seed of faith grows by hearing the Word of God. And let's not kid ourselves. Just as a seed left to itself will wither and die, so will your faith. Notice the word hearing is in that verse twice. The seed of faith is planted in the ground of our hearts by continually hearing the Word of God—reading the Bible, hearing biblical sermons at church, reading Spirit-inspired books, listening to Spirit-inspired music; our faith is built on hearing the Word of God.

If you're not used to taking your Bible into your prayer time, you should be. The best prayer is Scripture-filled prayer. If you put the seed of the Word of God into the soil of your heart, you'll reap a harvest as it pours out in prayer to bless God, to resist the devil, and to receive blessings for yourself and others.

Journal today how the scriptures you have been memorizing have helped you in your life.

_____

_____

_____

_____

_____

_____

_____

_____

_____

_____

_____

_____

_____

FULL ASSURANCE OF FAITH

"If we confess our sins, He is faithful and just to forgive us our sins and to cleanse us from all unrighteousness."
I John 1:9

"If we admit our sins—make a clean breast of them—he won't let us down; he'll be true to himself. He'll forgive our sins and purge us from all wrongdoing....I write this, dear children, to guide you out of sin. But if anyone does sin, we have a Priest-Friend in the presence of the Father: Jesus Christ, righteous Jesus. When he served as a sacrifice for our sins, he solved the sin problem for good—not only ours, but the whole worlds."
I John 1:9; 2:1–2, The Message

KEY STATEMENT: Complete obedience comes from the heart.

It's hard to come to God in full assurance of faith if you are living a life of disobedience. King Saul tried it. He stood before the great prophet and gave excuses. "I did most of what I was supposed to" may be acceptable in today's Western culture, but this is not acceptable to God. Yet, how could King David "get away" with adultery and worse? Wasn't he just as bad as Saul? The answer isn't complex. David was a man after God's own heart, but Saul turned back from God's heart (I Sam. 15:11).

Yes, Saul sinned, and yes, David sinned. But the fact of the matter lies within the motives of the heart. From persecution and living in caves, through countless battles and terrible family troubles to lofty days as king, David kept his heart aligned with God's heart. Even when his trouble was brought on by his own sin, he kept his heart bent toward God. David's wealth was never in lands, servants, or gold. Make no mistake about it; David found his riches in intimacy with God.

God isn't looking for perfection; He's looking for a servant's heart. You can't stay in sin and disobedience and fool yourself that you are a man like David. The way to deal with sin is to repent of it and flee from it. You can do that right now. If you have been struggling in an area and seem unable to overcome it, find a prayer partner who can also hold you accountable, or go to your pastor or a qualified Christian counselor. God isn't looking to condemn you; His heart is for you. Search your heart right now, ask God to show you areas of disobedience and immediately deal with it!

That is a word from God for you today. Write down and do what God shows you.

_____

_____

_____

_____

_____

FVLL ASSVRANCE OF FAITH

Week 11 Day 77

"And by this we know that we are of the truth, and shall assure our hearts before Him.
For if our heart condemns us, God is greater than our heart, and knows all things.
Beloved, if our heart does not condemn us, we have confidence toward God.
And whatever we ask we receive from Him, because we keep His commandments
and do those things that are pleasing in His sight."
1 John 3:19–22

KEY STATEMENT: God has good things for those whose hearts are yielded to Him.

We know we are of the truth not because we think so or hope we are. We certainly don't look to the world for the assurance of our faith. As we walk in obedience to Jesus' commandments, our hearts are assured by the witness of the Holy Spirit and the fellowship of the saints.

Thank God our standard is Jesus. If it were left up to us, we would either live lives of wild sin and self-deception, thinking we can waltz into God's presence regardless of the state of our heart, or we would go to the other extreme of legalism, always condemning ourselves and never having confidence before God.

Thank God He has given us the Holy Spirit whereby we can have intimacy with Jesus, the Living Word. It is the Holy Spirit who will keep us in balance.

End your week with this prayer:

Father God, thank You for the Holy Spirit and the Word. You knew me from eternity past. Before I was born, You knew my name. You've called me, anointed me, and appointed me for good things. I want to tell You that it is so great to fellowship with You now. Though You are the Lord of all creation, You are spending time with me right now, and I don't take that lightly. Transform me into a person after Your own heart. Teach me, lead me, comfort me, chastise me, and empower me. I so welcome all You have for me. You know me better than I know myself. Remind me of that. I yield to You. Let Your will be done in my life, not my will. I worship You.

_____

_____

_____

_____

_____

_____

_____

_____

FULL ASSURANCE OF FAITH

Additional Notes

DRAWING NEAR

"But seek first the kingdom of God and His righteousness, and all these things shall be added to you."
Matthew 6:33

"We live in an age disturbed, confused, bewildered, afraid of its own forces, in search not merely of its road but even of its directions. There are many voices of counsel, but few voices of vision; there is much excitement and feverish activity, but little concert of thoughtful purpose. We are distressed by our own ungoverned, undirected energies and do many things, but nothing long. It is our duty to find ourselves."
Woodrow Wilson, 1907

KEY STATEMENT: Put God's interests before yours, and He will see to it your needs are met.

Woodrow Wilson gave the words above in a baccalaureate address to Princeton University. Almost 100 years have passed, and nothing has changed. We are incapable of finding ourselves or direction on our own. We must be found of God. That is our highest duty.

What an amazing journey this has been and will continue to be. History is made; the world is changed every day by people like you. The list is long of those you will touch throughout the journey of your life. The arm of God has a long reach through you if you will be sensitive and respond to Him. Perhaps you've never fully considered it, but it is Him through you who will come to the aid of the disturbed, confused, bewildered, and afraid. You are God's answer to a hurting world.

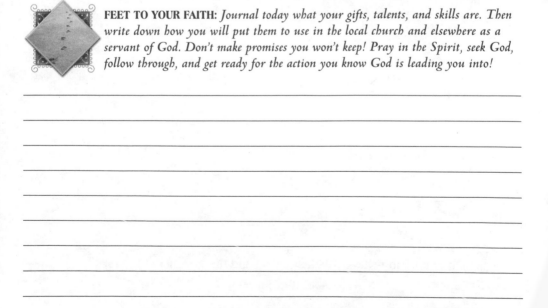

FEET TO YOUR FAITH: *Journal today what your gifts, talents, and skills are. Then write down how you will put them to use in the local church and elsewhere as a servant of God. Don't make promises you won't keep! Pray in the Spirit, seek God, follow through, and get ready for the action you know God is leading you into!*

DRAWING NEAR

"Jesus said to him, 'You shall love the LORD your God with all your heart, with all your soul, and with all your mind.' This is the first and great commandment. And the second is like it: 'You shall love your neighbor as yourself.' On these two commandments hang all the Law and the Prophets."
Matthew 22:37–40

"Observance of the Law, therefore, is not a work that our power can accomplish, but it is a work of a spiritual power. Through this spiritual power it is brought about that our hearts are cleansed from their corruption and are softened to obey unto righteousness." [16]
John Calvin, Instruction of Faith, 1537

KEY STATEMENT: It is a relationship we have with God through Christ, not just religious duty or law.

"Oh my," declared the young lady. "You've got to be kidding. You mean God already knows that I couldn't possibly keep all those laws and rules? I mean, I've tried to be good, but now you're telling me that the reason Jesus came was because I couldn't perfectly keep those commandments?" When the young pastor told her "yes" and then preached the simple truth of the gospel to her, she quickly became joyously saved.

- How do you reconcile the fact that one scripture tells you to be silent before God and another tells you to shout before the Lord?
- How do you reconcile the fear of God and keeping His commandments with the love of God and freedom in Christ?

Simple; it all hangs on one word: love. Love is about relationships, intimacy, partnership, giving, caring, selflessness, and passion. Take a lesson from one of the men who changed the world. Calvin's quote says it all.

Whenever you go to prayer, if you are sensitive to the Lover of your soul, you'll know when to shout and when to hold your tongue, when to act and when to be still. The beauty of it is love, a love that transcends all understanding.

_____

_____

_____

_____

_____

It is time to review "Week 2 day 8" and the "10 memory verses" of your journey.

DRAWING NEAR

Week 12, Day 80

"But in all things we commend ourselves as ministers of God: in much patience, in tribulations, in needs, in distresses, in stripes, in imprisonments, in tumults, in labors, in sleeplessness, in fastings; by purity, by knowledge, by longsuffering, by kindness, by the Holy Spirit, by sincere love, by the word of truth, by the power of God, by the armor of righteousness on the right hand and on the left, by honor and dishonor, by evil report and good report; as deceivers, and yet true; as unknown, and yet well known; as dying, and behold we live; as chastened, and yet not killed; as sorrowful, yet always rejoicing; as poor, yet making many rich; as having nothing, and yet possessing all things."
2 Corinthians 6:4–10

KEY STATEMENT: God's perspective is revealed as we are intimate with Him.

Born in Scotland about 1514, John Knox entered the Roman Catholic priesthood as the reformation in Germany and Switzerland was rising, but in his country it was mostly evident in its martyrs. Knox's friend and mentor George Wishart had been suspected of heresy because he read the New Testament with his students! Wishart fled Scotland but returned six years later, only to be arrested. Knox wouldn't leave his side until Wishart said, "One is sufficient for one sacrifice." The fire that burned Wishart at the stake lit a fire of reformation in the heart of John Knox.

Within a year of Knox being called by God to preach, he was taken prisoner in a siege to the castle of Saint Andrews. Contrary to the terms of surrender, he was confined to the galleys as a captive slave loaded with chains and forced to row the ships under the whips of the overseers. Released from the galleys about two years later, his health affected for the remainder of his life, the intrepid and passionate preacher became the uncompromising force behind the Scottish Reformation.

How different that story reads than what we are used to. We complain because we didn't get the promotion we saw as part of our life's journey. To finish the last semester for our beloved degree we had to take a second job for tuition. The tire went flat on the way to the sales meeting, and we lost our commission. We argued with our wife and "lost the anointing" for a Sunday sermon. God's perspective is what we need. Our journey is to be His journey, and, of course, like any great odyssey, it will be fraught with challenges, sorrows, victories, the unknown, offenses, and more. The only way you'll be up for the challenge is through the empowerment and proper perspective that comes with a life of intimacy with God.

In your prayer time today, ask God to give you some real perspective. It may be our situation is a whole lot better than we tend to complain about. God has some awesome, serious God-work for you to do. Let go of the temporary concerns and focus on your eternal purpose. (2 Cor. 4:17-18).

DRAWING NEAR

Week 12 Day 81

"Call to Me, and I will answer you, and show you great and mighty things, which you do not know."
Jeremiah 33:3

KEY STATEMENT: When God draws near to you, He reveals Himself and His ways.

There are different ways God will impart His thoughts to you when He draws near. It can be a strong voice in your heart that almost seems audible; but more often, it is a still, quiet voice deep within that leaves a lasting impression of His will. At other times, He may communicate through the world around us using another believer, a book, or music. Still at other times, God will powerfully reveal Himself through dreams and visions.

In whatever manner God speaks, it is always in perfect harmony with the Scriptures and is accompanied by an inner peace that will rule your heart. After each encounter, we are permanently transformed by the power of His presence. We are never the same.

Remember your flagship scripture, and look: Who draws near first? You do. In today's journaling, jot down a few notes of how God has changed you in the encounters you've had with Him during this journey.

_____

_____

_____

_____

_____

_____

_____

_____

_____

_____

_____

_____

_____

_____

_____

_____

DRAWING NEAR

Week 12 Day 82

"But it is good for me to draw near to God; I have put my trust in the Lord GOD, that I may declare all Your works."
Psalms 73:28

KEY STATEMENT: Intimacy with God brings trust in God.

This scripture declares it is good to draw near to God. Has it been? What exactly has been good, and what has been difficult or otherwise on this journey you have been taking? God already knows just where you stand, but as you are honest with Him the barriers to intimacy will crumble.

Embrace Him in trust because He loves you and cares for you exactly where you are as long as you turn your heart toward Him. If you've completed these 82 days, you've come a long way, and you have proven you have the substance of a strong believer.

In today's prayer and journaling, go ahead and practice what you've learned. Pour out your heart to God; sit with Him and fellowship, and let the Lord of life show you it's good for you to draw near.

_____
_____
_____
_____
_____
_____
_____
_____
_____
_____
_____
_____
_____
_____
_____
_____
_____

DRAWING NEAR

"'I will bring him near and he will come close to me, for who is he who will devote himself to be close to me?' declares the LORD."
Jeremiah 30:21 NIV

KEY STATEMENT: Intimacy with God is like a garden: the more you sow, the more you reap.

God looks for those who will devote themselves to Him. Of course, this is a devotional that you are using right now. Have you thought about what it means to be devoted to God? Although we can learn from the simple elegance of a faithful dog's devotion to its master or a subject's devotion to a king, these are not really what God is speaking of. The kind of devotion God desires is a blend of steadfast obedience and loving passion.

- **Obedience.** In sacred duty to our God and King, we willingly sacrifice self as we fight the good fight. We are not devoted because we feel like it or necessarily understand, but because His Word is to be obeyed for who He is and regardless of circumstance. The more we obey and see the blessed results of obedience, the more trust we develop, so we cultivate the godly habit of simple obedience.

- **Love.** We are not of this world so with holy passion we completely give ourselves to Him who is the Lover and Keeper of our souls. As we sow ourselves into God, He leads us, woos us, and captures our hearts; and we are drawn back to Him again and again. Hopelessly in love, endlessly enthralled, we grow in grace.

When you think of your relationship with the Lord like this, you see something wonderful happening. You realize that intimacy with God is almost self-perpetuating. In other words, the more you get, the more you'll want. The new wine of the Holy Spirit is truly addictive. God is a rewarder of those who diligently seek Him, and He has made the first move. Make sure you answer. Respond to the call of Him who gave you a voice and the very breath to answer! If we really knew the beauty of the One who awaits us, we'd fall over ourselves to go quickly, fiercely and jealously guarding our times of intimacy.

Think about that in today's devotional time. You are the bride of Christ. Devote your body, soul, and spirit solely to Him. You'll never be the same.

_____

_____

_____

_____

_____

_____

DRAWING NEAR

 *Week 12 Day 84*

"Now to Him who is able to keep you from stumbling, and to present you faultless before the presence of His glory with exceeding joy, to God our Savior, who alone is wise, be glory and majesty, dominion and power, both now and forever. Amen."
Jude 24–25

KEY STATEMENT: God has good things for those whose hearts are yielded to Him.

Like your first day, this is it. You are here at the end. The beginning and everything leading up to now is a memory. Yet again, at this very moment, it starts. Not this devotional journal, but the everyday epic of the rest of your life. Today is your lead-off in that race.

Eighty-four days ago this question was posed to you: what does this journey mean to me? In today's journal, rediscover the answer. You're a lot wiser today than you were twelve weeks ago. And if you haven't done so recently, look back over your journey; remember the potholes, the road blocks, the perseverance, the triumphs, and the tears as you have sought the face of God. You'll find some moments of incredible insight which will inspire you to continue journaling as you commune with God.

_____

_____

_____

_____

_____

_____

_____

_____

One thing we know: God is able to keep you and bring you into His presence with great joy. That's the promise from God in James 4:8.

Jesus is the same yesterday, today and forever (Heb. 13:8), so let's finish the same way we began. Take some time and bend your heart toward God. Consider His heavens, the beauty of His creation, and the awe-inspiring attributes of your Creator. Remember to be yourself; don't edit your worship or your prayers, and don't forget to thank Him and tell Him you are looking forward to tomorrow! Hallelujah! Glory to God!

Draw near to God and He will draw near to you!

"Drawing Near" Devotional Journal

Additional Notes

"Drawing Near" Devotional Journal

Additional Notes

"Drawing Near" Devotional Journal

Additional Notes

"Drawing Near" Devotional Journal

Additional Notes

_____
_____
_____
_____
_____
_____
_____
_____
_____
_____
_____
_____
_____
_____
_____
_____
_____
_____
_____
_____
_____
_____
_____
_____
_____
_____
_____
_____

Notes

1. Week 1, Day 7: From E. M. Bounds, Power Through Prayer (Grand Rapids, MI: Baker Books, 1991).

2. Week 4, Day 25: From Charles G. Finney, The Autobiography of Charles G. Finney (Minneapolis, MN: Bethany House Publishers, 1977).

3. Week 4, Day 26: From Colin C. Whittaker, Great Revivals (Springfield, MO: Gospel Publishing House, 1986).

4. Week 5, Day 32: From Bounds, Power Through Prayer.

5. Week 5, Day 32: Ibid.

6. Week 5, Day 34: Ibid.

7. Week 6, Day 37: From George Whitefield's journals.

8. Week 6, Day 38: From Whittaker, Great Revivals.

9. Week 7, Day 45: From Andrew Murray, Humility (Minneapolis, MN: Bethany House Publishers, 2001).

10. Week 7, Day 49: From Charles H. Spurgeon, The Quotable Spurgeon (Wheaton, IL: Harold Shaw Publishers, 2000).

11. Week 8, Day 55: From Andrew Murray, The Prayer Life (N.p.:, 1985).

12. Week 8, Day 56: From Spurgeon, The Quotable Spurgeon.

13. Week 9, Day 57: From Murray, The Prayer Life.

14. Week 9, Day 59: From Charles G. Finney, Revivals of Religion (N.p.).

15. Week 11, Day 73: From Great Voices of the Reformation (N.p.).

16. Week 12, Day 79: Ibid.

Your Journey never ends...

We hope this *Devotional Journal* has helped guide you as you continue
on the *life-long* adventure available to those who make the decision
to live each day in Intimacy with God.

Giving God glory...

If there is a personal story you would like to share about how this
Devotional Curriculum Kit has strengthened your relationship with God,
we would love to hear from you.
mail@johnbevere.org

Master Code Page

Please remember to watch for the icon to view the additional bonus content on these discs. If you wish to unlock additional content found in the Video Sessions; those codes can be found in the Student Workbook, which is available for purchase.

Introduction & Welcome

The first time you watch the DVD, please choose the "Individual" path. You will be asked to enter the code below for a personal welcome from John

DVD Extra Feature   Enter code: **564**, *to watch this bonus feature as you begin your journey.*

Your Drawing Near journey begins with a saving relationship with Jesus. Turn to page 237 and read Appendix A ("Our Need for a Savior") in your Drawing Near book.

Enter code: **297**, *to watch the bonus feature in the First Session of your DVD.**

DVD Extra Feature   *(*Please note that this code is for the 2nd bonus icon in session 1, not the first icon.)*

Enter code: **892**, *to watch this bonus feature in Session 5 of your DVD.*

DVD Extra Feature

Enter code: **792**, *to watch this bonus feature in Session 6 of your DVD.*

DVD Extra Feature

The next step on your journey to intimacy with the Holy Spirit is the infilling of the Holy Spirit in your life. Turn to page 241 and read Appendix B ("How to Be Filled With the Holy Spirit") in your Drawing Near book and enter code

Enter code: **767**, *to watch this bonus feature in Session 9 of your DVD.*

DVD Extra Feature

To reach us please call:
U.S. - 1-800-648-1477

Europe - 44 (0) 870-745-5790

Australia - 1-300-650-577 (outside AUS. +61 2 8850 1725)

Please contact us today to receive your free copy of Messenger International's newsletter and our 24 page color catalog of ministry resources!

The vision of MI is to strengthen believers, awaken the lost and captive in the church and proclaim the knowledge of His glory to the nations. John and Lisa are reaching millions of people each year through television and by ministering at churches, bible schools and conferences around the world. We long to see God's Word in the hands of leaders and hungry believers in every part of the earth.

 MESSENGER INTERNATIONAL

www.johnbevere.org
with John and Lisa Bevere

UNITED STATES
PO Box 888
Palmer Lake, CO 80133-0888
800-648-1477 (US & Canada)
Tel: 719-487-3000
Fax: 719-487-3300
E-mail: jbm@johnbevere.org

EUROPE
PO Box 622
Newport, NP19 8ZJ
UNITED KINGDOM
Tel: 44 (0) 870-745-5790
Fax: 44 (0) 870-745-5791
E-mail: jbmeurope@johnbevere.org

AUSTRALIA
PO Box 6200
Dural, D.C. NSW 2158
Australia
In AUS 1-300-650-577
Tel: +61 2 8850 1725
Fax +61 2 8850 1735
Email: jbmaustralia@johnbevere.org

The *Messenger* television program broadcasts in 214 countries. Some of the major networks include The God Digital Network in Europe, the Australian Christian Channel and on the New Life Channel in Russia. Please check your local listings for day and time.

D R A W I N G
N E A R

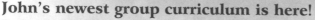

MULTIMEDIA CURRICULUM KIT

This kit contains John's newest hardcover book "Drawing Near",
Leader's Guide, Student Workbook, 5 VHS Tapes, 6 Audio CDs
and 4 DVDs with BRAND NEW Interactive Bonus Video Content. In
addition we have also added special Pastors/Leaders "Promotional Pack."

John's newest group curriculum is here!

**Perfect for church services, cell groups, bible studies, family studies, Christian schools
and Bible Colleges.**

This 12-week interactive video curriculum (featuring special messages filmed in the Rocky
Mountains) is a treasure map to the very heart of God. Rather than a mechanical or dry academic approach, your group will take a highly interactive relationship-based JOURNEY of
Drawing Near!

**New easy-to-lead style, and even easier
to follow, discover the keys to:**

- Entering into God's very presence
- Communicating with the Holy Spirit
- Unlocking the mysteries of God
- Developing a lifelong heart of worship

*You will see unity and power come to your church
or group as they are mightily strengthened and
awakened to the very nature of God. Travel
together to find the truth that you were created
to walk in intimacy with God Himself!*

THE PERFECT COMPANION
TO DRAWING NEAR

Intimacy with the Holy Spirit
2 Videos or 2 DVDs

Paul writes, "The communion (intimate fellowship) of the Holy Spirit be with you" (2 Cor. 13:14). Yet
so many do not enjoy this…why? As with all things in the Kingdom, we enter into this communion by faith. This faith is quickened by hearing His
Word on how He communicates with us. In
this important two-part series John addresses:
Is the infilling of the Holy Spirit for all? Is
the gift of tongues only for a select few? Why
even speak in tongues? The benefits of praying
in the Spirit. How God reveals His secrets.
How to communicate with God on His level
and much more!

These messages will ignite a passion and
bring understanding of how to have intimacy
with the Holy Spirit. It is a must for you and
those you love.

Our Special Edition "Intimacy with the Holy Spirit" DVD packaging comes with an attractive
custom shaped die cut package and holographic gold foil image on the case.